TUMBLING

VANNIE M. EDWARDS

Department of Physical Education,
Centenary College, Shreveport, Louisiana;
Coach, U.S. Olympic Team, Mexico City, 1968

795

ILLUSTRATED BY JAMES BONNER

W. B. SAUNDERS COMPANY
PHILADELPHIA • LONDON • TORONTO

W. B. Saunders Company: West Washington Square
Philadelphia, Pa. 19105

12 Dyott Street
London, WC1A 1DB

1835 Yonge Street
Toronto 7, Ontario

Saunders Physical Activities Series

Tumbling   SBN 0-7216-3335-8

Print No.:   9   8   7   6   5   4   3

SAUNDERS
PHYSICAL
ACTIVITIES
SERIES

Edited by

MARYHELEN VANNIER, Ed.D.
Professor and Director, Women's Division
Department of Health and Physical Education
Southern Methodist University

and

HOLLIS F. FAIT, Ph.D.
Professor of Physical Education
School of Physical Education
University of Connecticut

EDITORS' FOREWORD

Every period of history, as well as every society, has its own profile. Our own world of the last third of the twentieth century is no different. Whenever we step back to look at ourselves, we can see excellences and failings, strengths and weaknesses, that are peculiarly ours.

One of our strengths as a nation is that we are a sports-loving people. Today more persons — and not just young people — are playing, watching, listening to, and reading about sports and games. Those who enjoy themselves most are the men and women who actually *play* the game: the "doers."

You are reading this book now for either of two very good reasons. First, you want to learn — whether in a class or on your own — how to play a sport well, and you need clear, easy-to-follow instructions to develop the special skills involved. If you want to be a successful player, this book will be of much help to you.

Second, you may already have developed skill in this activity, but want to improve your performance through assessing your weaknesses and correcting your errors. You want to develop further the skills you have now and to learn and perfect additional ones. You realize that you will enjoy the activity even more if you know more about it.

In either case, this book can contribute greatly to your success. It offers "lessons" from a real professional: from an outstandingly successful coach, teacher, or performer. All the authors in the *Saunders Physical Activities Series* are experts and widely recognized in their specialized fields. Some have been members or coaches of teams of national prominence and Olympic fame.

This book, like the others in our Series, has been written to make it easy for you to help yourself to learn. The author and the editors want you to become more self-motivated and to gain a greater understanding of, appreciation for, and proficiency in the exciting world of *movement*. All the activities described in this Series — sports, games, dance, body conditioning, and weight and figure control activities — require skillful, efficient movement. That's what physical activity is all about. Each book contains descriptions and helpful tips about the nature, value, and purpose of an activity, about the purchase and care of equipment, and about the fundamentals of each movement skill involved. These books also tell you about common errors and how to avoid making them, about ways in which you can improve your performance, and about game rules and strategy, scoring, and special techniques. Above all, they should tell you how to get the most pleasure and benefit from the time you spend.

Our purpose is to make you a successful *participant* in this age of sports activities. If you are successful, you will participate often—and this will give you countless hours of creative and recreative fun. At the same time, you will become more physically fit.

"Physical fitness" is more than just a passing fad or a slogan. It is a condition of your body which determines how effectively you can perform your daily work and play and how well you can meet unexpected demands on your strength, your physical skills, and your endurance. How fit you are depends largely on your participation in vigorous physical activity. Of course no one sports activity can provide the kind of total workout of the body required to achieve optimal fitness; but participation with vigor in any activity makes a significant contribution to this total. Consequently, the activity you will learn through reading this book can be extremely helpful to you in developing and maintaining physical fitness now and throughout the years to come.

These physiological benefits of physical activity are important beyond question. Still, the pure pleasure of participation in physical activity will probably provide your strongest motivation. The activities taught in this Series are *fun*, and they provide a most satisfying kind of recreation for your leisure hours. Also they offer you great personal satisfaction in achieving success in skillful performance—in the realization that you are able to control your body and its movement and to develop its power and beauty. Further, there can be a real sense of fulfillment in besting a skilled opponent or in exceeding a goal you have set for yourself. Even when you fall short of such triumphs, you can still find satisfaction in the effort you have made to meet a challenge. By participating in sports you can gain greater respect for yourself, for others, and for "the rules of the game." Your skills in leadership and fellowship will be sharpened and improved. Last, but hardly least, you will make new friends among others who enjoy sports activities, both as participants and as spectators.

We know you're going to enjoy this book. We hope that it—and the others in our Series—will make you a more skillful and more enthusiastic performer in all the activities you undertake.

Good luck!

MARYHELEN VANNIER

HOLLIS FAIT

CONTENTS

Chapter I

THE NATURE AND PURPOSE OF THE SPORT 1

Chapter II

NEEDED EQUIPMENT AND ITS CARE 2

Chapter III

BASIC SKILLS 3

Elementary Tumbling.. 3

1. Forward Roll Tuck Position............................... 3
2. Forward Roll Extended Stand........................... 4
3. Forward Roll Tuck Jump.................................... 4
4. Forward Roll Walkout....................................... 6
5. Forward Straddle Leg Roll 8
6. Combination Forward Roll Tuck, Forward Roll
   Walkout, Forward Straddle Leg Roll............... 10
7. Standing Forward Roll Jump 10
8. Jump Half Twist 11
9. Standing Forward Roll Jump Half Twist 11
10. Forward Roll Jump Full Twist......................... 12
11. Back Roll Tuck 13
12. Back Roll Straddle Stand............................... 15
13. Back Roll Knee Scale...................................... 15
14. Back Roll Shoot to Knee Scale 17
15. Back Roll Shoot to Handstand......................... 18
16. Back Roll Jump with Half Twist 20
17. Combination Back Roll Straddle, Back Roll Tuck,
    Back Roll Shoot to Knee Scale 20

The Handstand 21

18. Handstand Forward Roll 21
19. Handstand Forward Roll Jump 23

20. Handstand Forward Roll Straddle Stand 24
21. Handstand Front Roll Jump with Half Twist 24
22. Combination Forward Roll Jump with Half Twist, Back Roll Jump with Half Twist, Forward Roll Straddle Stand 25
23. Combination Handstand Front Roll Jump with Half Twist, Back Roll Shoot to a Handstand Stepout, Front Roll Walkout 26
24. Front Roll with Straight Legs 27
25. Handstand Forward Roll Jump with Full Twist ... 29
26. Dive Forward Roll 29
27. Combination Handstand Forward Roll Jump with Full Twist, Dive Forward Roll...................... 30
28. Handstand Forward Straight Leg Roll................ 31
29. Combination Back Roll Jump with Half Twist, Dive Forward Roll, Handstand Forward Roll with Straight Legs 32

Acrobatics 33

30. Cartwheel... 33
31. Round-off 35
32. Back Bend... 37
33. Handstand Front Limber............................... 37
34. Front Walkover 38
35. Backover 40
36. Back Walkover 41
37. Front Tinsica.. 43
38. Combination Front Roll Walkout, Cartwheel, Back Roll Tuck 45
39. Combination Back Roll Extension Stepout, Cartwheel... 46
40. Back Tinsica.. 46
41. Front Limber, Front Roll Walkout, Cartwheel 47
42. Combination Front Limber, Front Roll Jump with Half Twist, Backover 48
43. Front Walkover, Cartwheel, Back Walkover......... 49
44. Combination Back Walkover with Half Turn, Front Walkover... 51
45. Combination Back Walkover Quarter Turn, Cartwheel Quarter Turn, Front Walkover............... 52
46. Combination Front Tinsica, Cartwheel, Back Walkover with Half Turn, Front Walkover........ 53
47. Combination Front Walkover, Cartwheel, Back Tinsica... 55
48. Combination Back Tinsica, Cartwheel 56

49. One-Arm Cartwheel with First Arm Down 57
50. One-Arm Cartwheel, Second Arm Down 59
51. Yogi Handstand................................. 59
52. Combination Cartwheel, One-Arm Cartwheel, Round-Off, Back Roll 61
53. One-Arm Front Walkover 63

Free Tumbling 64

54. Front Headspring... 64
55. Front Handspring... 66
56. Front Handspring Stepout............................... 68
57. Kangaroo Front Walkover............................... 70
58. Front Mounter 70
59. Combination Front Tinsica, One-Arm Cartwheel, Back Walkover... 71

Aerials 73

60. Aerial Cartwheel 73
61. Aerial Walkover 75
62. Back Handspring... 77
63. Combination Round-off, Back Handspring........... 79
64. Combination Front Handspring Stepout, Front Handspring... 80
65. Combination Cartwheel, Aerial Cartwheel 81
66. Combination Front Handspring Stepout, Round-off Back Handspring... 83
67. Combination Back Handspring, Back Handspring 84
68. Standing Back Somersault in Tucked Position...... 85
69. Front Somersault Tucked Position..................... 87
70. Front Somersault Stepout Position 89
71. Combination Front Handspring, Front Somersault 90
72. Combination Back Handspring, Back Somersault in Tucked Position 91
73. Combination Round-off, Back Handspring, Back Somersault in Tucked Position......................... 93
74. Combination Round-off, Back Handspring, Back Somersault in Layout Position 94
75. Combination Back Dive with a Half Twist, Forward Roll 95
76. Round-off Back Dive with a Half Twist, Forward Roll 96
77. Combination Round-off, Back Handspring, Back Dive with Half Twist, Forward Roll 97
78. Combination Front Somersault Stepout, Round-off, Back Handspring, Back Somersault Tuck 99
79. Back Somersault with Full Twist 101

80. Combination Round-off, Back Handspring, Back Somersault with Full Twist 103
81. Combination Round-off, Back Handspring, Back Somersault with Whip-back, Back Handspring... 104
82. Combination Round-off, Back Handspring, Back Somersault Whip-back, Back Handspring, Back Somersault in Tucked Position........................ 106

Chapter IV

RULES AND SCORING.. 109

Chapter V

TERMINOLOGY 110

Chapter VI

BIBLIOGRAPHY.. 112

Chapter VII

AVAILABLE FILM 113

I

THE NATURE AND PURPOSE OF THE SPORT

Tumbling is a vigorous activity involving strength, flexibility, agility, and power. The activity is basically a self-testing one, and the person makes progress at his own rate. It helps one develop motor coordination, body flexibility, self-discipline, and courage.

II
—
NEEDED EQUIPMENT
AND ITS CARE

Many equipment companies in the United States make tumbling mats, and there are as many variations in prices as there are in styles.

The most important points one must consider are the absorbability and the size of the mats. Those five by ten feet, preferably six by twelve, can be used crossways for the teaching of tumbling skills.

They should be cleaned before each workout. Most of them have a plastic water-proof cover and can be cleaned with soap and water.

III

BASIC SKILLS

ELEMENTARY TUMBLING

Elementary tumbling involves a front and back roll in which the body shows either a tuck, pike, or layout. The hands or feet are always in contact with the mat. Tumbling follows a proper sequence of skills. If the sequence is well chosen, every skill will lead into the next.

In most of the following skills, the spotter, whose responsibility is to protect you and to facilitate a skill, stands slightly behind you near your side. A few exceptions when he stands in a different area are mentioned in the text.

1. Forward Roll Tuck Position

Squatting on the mat, place your hands in front of your feet and six inches away from them with your fingers pointing ahead. Tuck your head, place your chin on your chest, and round your shoulders and back. Then allow your hands to leave the floor and grasp your shins. Be sure that your head remains close to your knees and your feet close to your seat to make a small base. Come up the back side and return to the low squat position.

Common Errors:

(1) Not using your arms to support your body weight on the first part of the roll. (2) Not keeping the body in a tight tuck throughout the roll.

Coaching Points:

(1) Remember your hand placement and the part your arms play on the first phase of the roll. (2) Be sure that your head remains on your chest and close to your knees and that your feet are close to your seat.

3

Practice Hints:

(1) Assume the correct starting position for the roll with your hands in place, chin tucked, and back rounded. (2) Lie on your back pulling your knees to your chest and roll up on your shoulders. Come down and forward to a standing position.

Spotting Tips:

The spotter stands in front of you. As you lower your head and start the roll, he places his hands on your hips and lifts them as your head passes under.

2. Forward Roll Extended Stand

From a squat position on the mat, place your hands on it in front of your feet and six inches from them with your fingers pointing ahead. Tuck your head and place your chin on your chest as you round your shoulders and back. Push off with your legs and roll forward. As you come out of the roll and your feet make contact with the mat, let your head and shoulders continue slightly forward while your hands release your shins and begin lifting forward and up to the vertical position. As your arms make their pattern up, straighten your legs.

Common Errors:

(1) Opening up before your knees, hips, and shoulders are over your feet. (2) Not having proper arm lift patterns as they extend up in the vertical position.

Coaching Points:

(1) Keep your head and feet in a tight tuck. (2) Upon standing, be sure that your arms travel in front of your body up to the vertical as you extend your legs.

Practice Hints:

(1) From a squat position, slowly practice the standing process with the proper arm patterns and leg extensions. Be sure your arms and legs are coordinated. (2) Do not aid yourself with your hands in the stand-up out of the roll.

Spotting Tips:

As you come out of the roll and begin to stand, the spotter places his hands on your hips and aids you in standing.

3. Forward Roll Tuck Jump

From a squat position on the mat, place your hands on the mat in front of your feet. Tuck your head by placing your chin on your

chest as you round your shoulders and back. Push off with your legs and roll forward. As you come out of the roll, swing your arms up and extend your legs with a vigorous action lifting your body in a vertical direction.

Common Errors:

(1) Not having proper use of your arms and head as you jump. (2) Not jumping in the right direction.

Coaching Points:

(1) Be sure that your arm patterns come from your sides and up in front of your body to the vertical position above your head as you focus your eyes up. (2) Jump straight up. (3) Do not arch your back.

Practice Hints:

(1) Upon completion of the roll, try to jump up and come down in the same spot from where you took off. (2) Jumping, try to touch a higher object each time. (3) From a squat postion, jump for height and control.

Spotting Tips:

As you come out of the roll, the spotter places his hands on your hips and lifts them up. As he assists you, he needs to be close enough that the lifting and balancing are coordinated with your body movement.

4. Forward Roll Walkout

Squat down on the mat and place your hands about six inches in front of your knees. Tuck your chin on your chest, and place your head on your knees as you begin the forward roll. Halfway over, straighten one leg to form a pike position. Allow the other leg to remain tucked with your heel close to your seat. Upon completion of the roll, walk out of it.

Common Errors:

(1) Not allowing your leg to remain straight. (2) Not producing enough velocity in the roll to come up to the walkout position without using your hands to push off the floor. (3) Having poor direction of the forward roll from the beginning.

Coaching Points:

(1) Flex your thigh muscle in the straight leg to prevent the leg from bending. (2) Be sure your back is rounded. (3) Give a firm push off the mat with your legs and toes. (4) Be sure your shoulders are square as they begin the first phase of the roll.

Practice Hints:

(1) In practicing the walkout, lie on your back and pull your legs back over your head to simulate the last half of the roll. Keep one leg straight, tuck the other one, and practice coming up to a stand. (2)

Practice a very rapid tucked forward roll to a stand; then try the walkout. (3) Use your arms to come up to the stride standing position by swinging them forward in front of your body up to the vertical. (4) Begin the roll from a standing position.

Spotting Tips:

The spotter faces you. As you complete the forward roll, he reaches forward and extends both arms to assist you as you attempt the walkout. Reach for his hands and use them to help yourself up.

5. Forward Straddle Leg Roll

From a standing position, bend forward at the waist placing your hands forward at shoulder level. Be sure to use your arms to let your head and back down. As your back touches half way over in the roll, part your legs wide. Keep your chin on your chest and tuck your head forward. When your feet make contact with the mat, place your hands between your legs. As your body weight comes over the base, push up and back with your arms and come to a low straddle stand.

Common Errors:

(1) Not parting your legs wide enough. (2) Not placing your hands between your legs as you come out of the roll. (3) Not thrusting your head and shoulders forward as you come to the straddle stand.

Coaching Points:

(1) Part your legs as wide as possible after you have completed the first part of the roll. (2) Be sure your hands are between your legs near the crotch. (3) Be sure your head and shoulders work with momentum as you attempt to bring your body weight over the base.

Practice Hints:

(1) Work a low straddle stand by itself, stretching for flexibility. (2) Work the last half of the roll from the back, up to the straddle stand. (3) From a straddle sitting position on the floor, snap your head and shoulders forward and press your arms down attempting to arrive at the straddle stand.

Spotting Tips:

As you come out of the forward roll, the spotter assists you in going into the straddle position by lifting your hips and pushing slightly forward.

6. Combination Forward Roll Tuck, Forward Roll Walkout, Forward Straddle Leg Roll

In the forward roll tuck, protect your head with your hands and remain in a tight tuck until your body weight is well over your feet and until you start into the forward roll walkout. Open one leg after the first half of the walkout roll. Keep enough momentum for the proper direction as you walk out to start the straddle leg roll. When coming up, part your legs as wide as possible and thrust your head and shoulders forward while you push with your arms between your legs.

Common Errors:

(1) Not mastering the individual skills. (2) Not having proper direction in the forward roll walkout. (3) Not parting your legs wide enough on the straddle role.

Coaching Points:

(1) Review the individual skills before you combine them. (2) Do the first two skills several times before you add the straddle leg roll.

Practice Hints:

(1) Review the individual skills daily. (2) Master every phase of the combination before learning a new skill.

Spotting Tips:

These have been covered under each separate skill.

7. Standing Forward Roll Jump

From a standing position, bend forward at the waist, placing your hands slightly in front of your shoulders on the mat. Tuck your chin on your chest and duck your head as you round your back. Push off with your feet and continue into a forward roll tuck. Just before your body weight comes over the base, begin to open your body as your arms swing forward and up to a vertical position. Thrust out your legs and lift your body high in the vertical. Try to go straight up and land from where you took off. Upon landing, bend your legs slightly to absorb the shock. Return to a straight stand.

Common Errors:

(1) Opening before the center of gravity is over the base. (2) Not using your arms properly in jumping. (3) Having your head down instead of up.

Coaching Points:

(1) Jump to gain height in the vertical direction. (2) Make sure

your arms are coordinated with your jump. (3) Cast your eyes up on the jump to use your kinesthetic sense for body location.

Practice Hints:

(1) Do the jump from a low squat position, landing from where you took off. (2) Use a leap meter to measure progress of jumps. (3) Remember the importance of jumping and its relationship to other activities. (4) Fix your eyes on a particular object as you attempt to jump, turn, or land.

Spotting Tips:

As you complete the roll, the spotter lifts your hips. He must be fast, for this movement is fast.

8. Jump Half Twist

From a standing position on the mat, bend your legs to a semi-squat position. As your arms swing up, allow either arm to swing obliquely across the body as you look in the direction of the throwing arm, creating a half spiral rotation of your body as it is suspended. Upon landing, allow your arms to come down to shoulder height horizontally.

Common Errors:

(1) Throw your arm horizontally rather than obliquely. (2) Looking opposite to the arm throw. (3) Starting the twist before your feet leave the mat.

Coaching Points:

(1) Do the arm and head mechanics without the jump. (2) Attempt to suspend your body before starting the twist. (3) Focus your eyes ahead when landing.

Practice Hints:

(1) Practice your head and arm directions in front of a mirror. (2) Try to get maximum height and land in the same place from which you jumped. (3) Motivate yourself by realizing the many uses the jump and twist have in all areas of sports.

Spotting Tips:

The spotter places his hands on your hips. As you jump, he lifts up to turn your body in the direction of the twist. His hands release your hips and slide loosely around your body to assist you in landing.

9. Standing Forward Roll Jump Half Twist

Standing, bend forward at the waist and place your hands on the mat slightly in front of your shoulders. Tuck your head and round your back as the roll begins. When your body weight is over the base, extend your arms and legs coming up. Swing either arm obliquely, looking in the same direction to execute the half twist. As you land, gain your balance by putting your arms parallel to the floor and out to the side.

Common Errors:

(1) Starting the jump too soon before your body weight is over your feet. (2) Throwing your arms horizontally rather than up and obliquely. (3) Not having proper arm throw, preventing your feet from landing under your body.

Coaching Points:

(1) Be sure your body weight is well over the base when starting the jump. (2) Remember that correct arm-throw patterns are essential for proper body position on the twist. (3) Keep your legs and feet together during the jump and twist action, allowing them to part on landing.

Practice Hints:

(1) Practice proper arm direction in front of a mirror. (2) Attempt the jump with a half twist as an isolated skill. (3) Be sure your body weight is in proper position before you jump.

Spotting Tips:

As you complete the forward roll, the spotter places his hands on your hips pushing left or right, depending upon the direction you twist. After he lifts and pushes, he releases your hips and straightens his arms around your body to help you in landing.

10. Forward Roll Jump Full Twist

From a standing position, do a tuck forward roll. As your body weight comes over the base, swing either arm up and across your body obliquely while the other arm swings straight above your head. Follow the oblique arm direction with your head as you do a full twist, keeping your legs and feet together. Part your legs just before you land on the mat as your arms come to the side horizontally for balance on landing.

Common Errors:

(1) Starting the twist too soon while your feet are still on the mat. (2) Having improper arm direction on your thrust. (3) Not coordinating your total body movement throughout the skill.

Coaching Points:

(1) Remember that the full twist does not take much more effort than the half twist. (2) Be sure to use proper arm directions on the twist. (3) Keep all body segments working together.

Practice Hints:

(1) Attempt to do the jump and full turn without the forward roll. (2) Try to do the full turn and land in the same spot from which you started. (3) Do this skill in front of a mirror often in order to see your own mistakes.

Spotting Tips:

As you come out of the forward roll, the spotter places his hands on your hips to assist your jumping and twisting. As you twist, his hand slips from your waist and goes loosely around your body to steady you upon landing.

11. Back Roll Tuck

From a squatting position with your back to the mat, tuck your chin on your chest. Place your head forward and round your back, putting your hands on the mat just in front of your knees. Push off from the mat and roll back. As your hands push off from the mat, place them beside your head. When your hands make contact with the mat behind your head, push. Keep your knees tucked in to your chest. As you come out of the roll, land on your feet, not your knees.

Common Errors:

(1) Not keeping your neck and back rounded in the first part of the roll. (2) Not having proper hand placement by your head on the roll. (3) Not pushing off equally with both arms as the roll goes over the top.

Coaching Points:

(1) Remember that your back, neck and shoulder form a rocker. (2) Remember the function of your hands and arms. As soon as your hands leave the mat in the beginning of the roll, put them by your head. (3) Keep a tight tuck and land on both feet, not your knees.

Practice Hints:

(1) From a starting position with your head and back rounded, rock in a tuck doing a half roll in order to feel the rocker action. (2) In the rocker exercise, place your hands by your head as you roll back.

Spotting Tips:

As you roll back and place your hands on the mat beside your head, the spotter lifts your hips as your body rolls over your head.

12. Back Roll Straddle Stand

Standing with your back to the mat, squat down, flexing your knees while placing your hands slightly behind your hips. Round your back and shoulders, and tuck your chin to your chest. Continue the backward momentum by rolling back. Be sure that your hands move from behind your hips to the side of your neck and that they help lift your body as it goes over your head. As soon as your hands and head touch the mat going back, part your legs wide. Land in a straight-leg straddle.

Common Errors:

(1) Failing to lower your body gently from a standing to a squat position. (2) Placing your arms by your head too late. (3) Parting your legs too late so that they are not straight.

Coaching Points:

(1) Bend your knees first, then bend your trunk forward at the waist to lower your body to a low squat position. (2) Be sure your arms are down on the first phase. (3) Spread your legs as soon as your hands and head touch the mat.

Practice Hints:

(1) Practice coming from a standing position to a low squat, then to a roll position without stopping. (2) From a half head stand, spread your legs, push with your arms and come up to a straddle stand.

Spotting Tips:

As you start the back roll straddle, the spotter lifts your hips as your body passes over your head and neck. He lets you know when your arms push in coming over in the roll.

13. Back Roll Knee Scale

From a low squat position, tuck your head, round your back, and roll back over your head. As your hands and head touch the mat, extend one leg fully and allow the other one to remain tucked. Upon landing on your toes, straighten your arms. On the tucked leg, from the toes, lower to your shin then to your knee. Lower the extended leg horizontally to the mat. Put your arms at a 90 degree angle to your chest and the extended leg at 90 degrees to the other leg. Look up.

Common Errors:

(1) Failing to extend the straight leg. (2) Landing too heavily on your toes and lowering too hard to your knees. (3) Not showing proper body angles in the final rest on the mat.

Coaching Points:

(1) Maintain good direction on the back roll. (2) Push hard with your arms to lift your body on the head roll. (3) Extend one leg as

Back Roll Knee Scale

soon as your hands and head touch the mat in the back roll. (4) Keep your other leg tucked. (5) Lower to the scale position gently.

Practice Hints:

(1) Perfect the back roll before adding the scale. (2) Do push-ups to strengthen your arms. (3) From the squat head stand, extend one leg and tuck the other, doing the last half of the knee scale.

Spotting Tips;

As you come out of the back roll, the spotter grasps your extended leg with one hand, and places the other one on your stomach as he lowers your body into a knee scale.

14. Back Roll Shoot to Knee Scale

From a standing position, bend your knees and sit back as your trunk bends forward. Round your back and tuck your head. Place your hands behind your hips to lower your body as you begin the back roll. As your hands and head touch the mat going over into the roll, push and extend your hips vigorously. Split your legs, one going forward and the other one back. Lower your body, placing the rear leg down first by lowering it from your toe to your shin and then your knee. Lower the other leg to a horizontal position on the mat.

Common Errors:

(1) Failing to extend your hips and push your arms as your legs split. (2) Not having proper direction of your legs when they split. (3) Not raising your head. (4) Landing too heavily on the toe of your leading foot.

Coaching Points:

(1) As soon as your hands and head touch the mat, extend your hips and push with your arms. (2) As soon as your head clears the mat, look up and forward. (3) Control your body by leaning forward with your shoulders and gently lower your first foot.

Practice Hints:

(1) See a demonstration of right and wrong techniques. (2) Practice kicking a half handstand and lowering to a knee scale. (3) Try to show a crotch split of 180 degrees on the mat and in the handstand.

Spotting Tips:

As your hands and head touch the mat going back, the spotter grasps the extended leg with one hand and lifts your body up in the vertical direction. He places his other hand under your stomach helping to give your body proper direction on the down flight. He lowers your body to a finished knee scale.

15. Back Roll Shoot to Handstand

From a stand, sit back and bend your knees and hips. Round your back and tuck your head. Place your hands behind your hips as you lower your body. As you place your hands on the mat by your head, extend your hips and push your feet up to the vertical while you straighten your arms and bring your head up. Reach for a vertical handstand with your body. Break your body at your hips and snap them down, landing on both feet at the same time.

Common Errors:

(1) Not extending your legs to the vertical. (2) Failing to push your arms and extend your hips at the same time. (3) Not having your head up going into the handstand.

Coaching Points:

(1) Aim your feet in a vertical direction as your head and hands touch the mat. (2) Remember that you lift your hips and push your arms at the same time. (3) Raise your head as you reach the handstand.

Practice Hints:

(1) From a position on your back—hands by your head, fingers pointing toward your toes, feet over your head in a pike position—extend your legs up to a vertical position and push with your arms as your hips extend. (2) Let a partner hold your legs in a handstand and do inverted push ups.

Spotting Tips:

As you roll back and your hands touch the mat behind your head, the spotter grasps your legs as they shoot up to the vertical. He lifts up to help you gain control in the handstand.

Back Roll Shoot to Handstand

19

16. Back Roll Jump with Half Twist

From a standing position with your back to the mat, sit back placing your hands beside your hips to assist in lowering your body. Tuck your chin, round your back, and roll back. Place your hands beside your head as you start the back roll. Push with them as your body passes over your head, lifting your body weight off your neck. Stay in a tucked position until your feet touch the mat. Jump straight up making a half twist. After the jump, bring your arms from above your head horizontally to the side to assist in landing.

Common Errors:

(1) Failing to push with your arms as your body passes over your head. (2) Jumping too soon before the body weight comes over the base. (3) Beginning the half twist too soon to prevent your getting maximum altitude on the jump.

Coaching Points:

(1) Use a lightly inclined mat, and roll down it to help establish enough momentum for a good roll. (2) Twist at the height of the jump, making sure it is done in a vertical plane.

Practice Hints:

(1) Practice back roll stand. As you stand, come up on your toes. (2) Be sure your arm-lifting action is forward and up, coordinating it with your body.

Spotting Tips:

As you begin the back roll, the spotter places his hands on your hips and lifts your body as it passes over your head. As you jump, he lifts your hips up to help you twist.

17. Combination Back Roll Straddle, Back Roll Tuck, Back Roll Shoot to Knee Scale

As you move smoothly from one skill to the other, be sure you tuck your chin and round your shoulders and back. Push with your hands as your body passes over your head. Do the straddle and knee scale on the last half of each roll.

Common Errors:

(1) Failing to round your shoulders and to make your back a rocker for the first half of the roll. (2) Not having adequate push with your arms as your body passes over your head. (3) Beginning the straddle or knee scale too soon.

Coaching Points:

(1) Remember to establish a rocker with your back and head before starting the roll. (2) As soon as your hands touch the mat beside

your head, push to protect your neck. (3) Do the leg position as soon as your body passes the vertical.

Practice Hints:

(1) Looking in a mirror, observe your head, shoulders, and back at the beginning of the roll. (2) Have the spotter say "hup" when he lifts your hips. At this moment, push with your arms lifting your body up high.

Spotting Tips:

The spotter anticipates each new movement and is ready to assist you. His lifting of your hips as your body weight passes over your head is important.

THE HANDSTAND

The handstand is a basic skill which all good tumblers master. Learning how to recover from this skill is as important as learning how to hold one's body supported by his hands in an upright position.

The following sequence for learning and teaching the handstand is effective.

18. Handstand Forward Roll

Begin from a track start position. Run into the handstand by thrusting your rear leg up and straight toward the vertical. As you do this, lock your arms and keep your head up. Have your other leg follow the first, allowing them to come together over your hands. Keep your body in an extended vertical position and balance on your hands. In recovering, allow your feet to travel forward until they are ahead of your body and well over your hands. Gradually lower your head by slightly bending your arms and slowly piking your hips. Tuck your head under just before it touches the mat, round your shoulders, and roll down the back of your neck and back. Tuck your legs tightly and draw your feet close to your seat. Come up to a standing position lifting your arms up.

Common Errors:

(1) Placing your hands in front of your shoulders in the beginning. (2) Ducking your head and bending your arms and hips as you kick up. (3) Not allowing your legs to travel beyond the vertical on your recovery.

Coaching Points:

(1) Be sure the track start and hand placement positions are correct before you attempt the first part of the handstand. (2) Use your head and finger tips to adjust the balance of your body while in a

Handstand Forward Roll

handstand. (3) Be sure that your legs travel beyond the vertical before your arms and hips bend in the recovery from the forward roll.

Practice Hints:

(1) Kick up to a handstand against a wall. Be sure you straighten your arms and keep your head up. Push off the wall with your feet, returning them to the mat. (2) Stack mats on a tumbling pad. Do a handstand on the tumbling pad and recover by rolling into the stack of mats. Be sure your hands are placed six to eight inches away from the stack to allow room for your head in the recovery.

Spotting Tips:

The spotter grasps your first leg and lifts it. His other hand catches your other leg as it comes up. If your body sags, he reminds you to straighten it. He pulls your legs forward and over the base, checking to be sure that your arms do not bend and that you do not tuck your head too soon. He gradually lowers your body after you have ducked your head.

19. Handstand Forward Roll Jump

Begin from a track start position. Tuck one leg under your chest and bend the other one half way. Keep your arms straight and your head up as you kick your legs toward the vertical. Let your legs pass the vertical before you bend your arms slightly and lower your body. Bend your hips slightly toward a pike position and, as your back touches the mat, tuck your legs tightly. Keep your head forward until your body is well over your feet. Extend your legs and swing your arms up to a vertical position as you jump off the mat.

Common Errors:

(1) Failing to reach an extended handstand before beginning the forward roll. (2) Having a loose tuck coming out of the roll for the jump.

Coaching Points:

(1) Keep your arms straight as you kick into the handstand. (2) Be sure that you have your feet ahead of your hands before you go into the roll. (3) Tuck your body tightly as you begin the roll.

Practice Hints:

(1) Practice the handstand against a wall to develop a good one. (2) Use stacked mats to protect your neck when you roll out of the handstand. (3) Lie on your back and roll up on your shoulders, bringing your knees to your chest. Coming out of the roll, practice the jump.

Spotting Tips:

As you kick up, the spotter grasps your first leg with one hand and your second one with his other hand. He lifts your body to help you reach an extended handstand, with your legs passing the vertical as he lowers your head and shoulders forward to the mat.

20. Handstand Forward Roll Straddle Stand

Facing the mat, begin from a track start position, placing your hands in front of your first foot and behind your shoulders. Keep your arms straight and your head up. Kick your legs to a vertical position. Continue the movement of your legs beyond the vertical as you bend your arms and tuck your head under, lowering your body for the forward roll. As soon as you roll on your back, spread your legs wide and continue rolling forward. Coming out of the roll, place your hands between your legs and push up and back as you snap your head forward, moving in the direction of the roll.

Common Errors:

(1) Failing to reach the extended vertical position of the handstand before starting the forward roll. (2) Parting the legs too little when coming out of the roll. (3) Placing your hands improperly when coming up to the straddle stand.

Coaching Points:

(1) Lean your shoulders forward as you kick into the handstand. (2) Let your legs start a downward motion of the forward roll to help gain momentum. (3) Spread your legs wide when coming to a straddle stand.

Practice Hints:

(1) Do handstand rolls on a stack of mats. (2) Practice coming into a straddle stand from the position on your back. (3) Sit in a straddle position on a mat, bend forward at the trunk, and keep your legs straight.

Spotting Tips:

As you kick your legs to a handstand, the spotter grasps your legs and lifts them to check whether you are getting full extension in the handstand. He carries your legs forward beyond the vertical and helps lower you to a handstand. As you go into the forward roll, he releases you and steps behind to lift your hips as they come up into the straddle stand.

21. Handstand Front Roll Jump with Half Twist

From a track start position, kick into a handstand by locking your arms and holding your head up. Bring one leg up, then the other.

Allow them to continue over the top and beyond the vertical. Bend your arms, bring your shoulders forward, duck your head, and roll down the back of your neck to a rounded position. Come up to a standing position. As your feet touch the mat and your body weight comes over the base, extend your legs and swing your arms up obliquely, looking in the direction you are twisting. Complete the half twist and finish in a standing balanced position.

Common Errors:

(1) Failing to reach the stretched vertical position of the handstand. (2) Starting the roll too soon. (3) Trying to jump too soon and throwing your arms and head in the same direction.

Coaching Points:

(1) Master the handstand forward roll on a stack of mats. (2) Be sure your legs and hips pass beyond the vertical before you start the forward roll. (3) Throw your arms up obliquely, looking in the same direction.

Practice Hints:

(1) Practice the forward roll jump with a half twist. (2) Keep your head up as your feet and hips move forward out of the handstand. (3) Do not tuck your head under until the last second.

Spotting Tips:

The spotter grasps your first leg as you bring it up, then grasps the other one. He stretches you as you extend your body in a handstand, and holds your feet until you duck your head and put your shoulders on the mat. He then helps you jump and twist by placing his hands on your hips as you do so.

22. Combination Forward Roll Jump with Half Twist, Back Roll Jump with Half Twist, Forward Roll Straddle Stand

In the forward roll, remember to tuck your chin and round your back. Keep your feet in close to your seat when coming out of the roll. Swing your arms up obliquely, looking in the direction you twist. Round your back and place your hands beside your head for the back roll, taking the pressure off your neck. On the forward roll, spread your legs half way through the roll. Be sure to place your hands between your legs. Push up and back as you come out of the straddle stand.

Common Errors:

(1) Tucking too loosely when coming out of the roll. (2) Attempting to jump before your body weight is far enough over the base. (3) Not having proper arm patterns when jumping and twisting.

Coaching Points:

(1) In coming out of the roll in the tuck position, maintain a proper distance relationship from your chest to your knees and from your feet to your seat. (2) Look in the direction in which you are twisting. (3) Keep your body moving throughout the skill.

Practice Hints:

(1) In executing the series, do one skill at a time. (2) Relate the individual skill techniques to the complete series and move smoothly. (3) Be always conscious of form and body rhythm.

Spotting Tips:

The spotter moves with each part of the combination and should be ready to assist you when needed.

23. Combination Handstand Front Roll Jump with Half Twist, Back Roll Shoot to a Handstand Stepout, Front Roll Walkout

You must do each skill correctly in order for the next series to be done properly. In the handstand, let your legs follow the forward motion coming out of the handstand. Tuck tightly in the forward roll and jump with a twist, landing back in the same spot. Sit back gradually, placing your hands beside your head as your body weight passes over your head. Be sure your hips come in line over your feet before you jump and twist. Tuck your head under; and after the roll has progressed forward to your shoulders and back, bend one leg at your knee and straighten your other leg, coming into a walkout position.

Common Errors:

(1) Starting the forward roll from the handstand too soon. (2) Not allowing the jumps with the twist to be taken up, causing you to lose your balance. (3) Not remembering the proper position for the walkout in the forward roll walkout.

Coaching Points:

(1) Stretch your body fully while in a handstand position. (2) Watch your arm lift and throw patterns in the two half twists. (3) Point your toes and use good form.

Practice Hints:

(1) Work each skill separately until you have mastered it. (2) Use your finger tips and head to adjust your body in the handstand. (3) Practice executing just the jump with a half twist.

Spotting Tips:

The spotter stands to the side in front of you. He bends his knees ready to assist you in any phase of the series.

24. Front Roll with Straight Legs

From a standing position facing the mats, bend forward at your hips and place your hands on the mats. Tuck your chin on your chest and round your shoulders as you push off with your feet and lean forward going into the roll. Use your arms to lower the top of your body. As you come out of the forward roll, keep your legs together and straight. When your seat touches the mat coming out of the roll, place your hands beside your legs between your hips and knees. Push forward and up as your head and shoulders snap forward adding to the momentum of your body coming up and out of the roll. Finish in a stretched stand with your arms above your head.

Common Errors:

(1) Doing the first part of the roll too slowly and not building up momentum. (2) Failing to push with your hands when coming out of the roll. (3) Not having coordinated movements of your head, shoulders, and body on the last phase of the skill.

Coaching Points:

(1) Do the first part of the roll smoothly and rapidly. (2) Place your hands properly when coming up and out of the roll. (3) Be sure your head and upper trunk snap forward to help your body come up over your hips and straight legs to a stand.

Practice Hints:

(1) Stack several mats and do forward rolls on them, allowing your feet to land on the original mat. (2) Work on the flexibility of your trunk.

Spotting Tips:

As you roll forward, the spotter steps behind you and lifts your hips as you come out of the roll into a standing position.

Front Roll with Straight Legs

25. Handstand Forward Roll Jump with Full Twist

Begin from a track start position. Keep your arms straight and your head up as you kick your legs up to a vertical position in a handstand. Stretch your body in the handstand and allow your legs to continue forward and down until they have passed beyond your hands. Lower your head and shoulders gradually by bending your arms, tucking your chin on your chest, and rolling down on the back of your neck. As the back of your neck makes contact with the mat, tuck your legs and continue forward until your weight is over your feet. Extend your legs and swing your arms up obliquely and to the side. Look in the direction you twist. Do one full turn as you jump into the air and land in the same place from which you jumped.

Common Errors:

(1) Beginning the forward roll before reaching the handstand. (2) Tucking your legs too late as your body comes down from the handstand to the forward roll. (3) Having improper direction of your head and your arm throw while doing the full twist.

Coaching Points:

(1) Keep momentum going when coming out of the forward roll. (2) From a standing position, do a jump with a full twist and return to a standing position. (3) Check the position of your head direction and arm throw.

Practice Hints:

(1) Stack several mats on top of some tumbling pads to create a downhill slope. (2) Do a handstand on the stacked mats, rolling down on the slope to add momentum to the forward roll. (3) From a standing position, practice jumping with a full twist.

Spotting Tips:

As you kick into the handstand, the spotter grabs your legs with his hands. While you are in this position, he checks your back and lifts up if it is sagging. He pulls your legs forward beyond the vertical position to establish the forward motion. He holds your legs up and checks the bending of your arms and the ducking of your head before he releases your legs and allows you to roll down. As you jump, he places his hands on your hips and assists you by lifting up and helping your body twist. His hands slip off your waist as you turn. He holds you as you complete it.

26. Dive Forward Roll

From a standing position at the end of the mat, flex your knees and jump, swinging your arms up. Hold your head in line with your body. With your body in a loose pike position, dive up and slightly out. Using your arms as a shock absorber, gently lower your body. Be sure that your hips are traveling forward so that they pass over your hands quickly. Tuck your head and round your back so that you finish the roll gently. Tuck your legs when coming to a standing position.

Common Errors:

(1) Traveling out and low in the dive. (2) Having your hips too far behind the base as your hands come down out of the roll to make contact with the mat.

Coaching Points:

(1) Go up on the dive, not out. (2) Be sure that your head is tucked under and your arms support your body weight. (3) Maintain a tucked position when coming out of the forward roll.

Practice Hints:

(1) Use several layers of mats. (2) Remind yourself to lift up for height, not to dive out. (3) Do a short dive first, then build up to longer ones.

Spotting Tips:

After you dive into the cradled arms of the spotter, he gradually lowers you. He also checks your body position and hand placements when you come out of the dive into the roll.

27. Combination Handstand Forward Roll Jump with Full Twist, Dive Forward Roll

From a standing position at the end of the mat, get into a track start position. Keep your arms straight and your head up as you kick your legs up into a handstand. Allow your legs to pass beyond the vertical and to start down as you bend your arms and duck your head coming into a forward roll. As your body weight passes over your feet, extend your legs and swing your arms up obliquely. Look in the same direction as you throw your arms, executing a full twist. Upon landing, dive up as you pike your body by pushing from your legs and swinging your arms up. Keep your head in line with the upper part of your body. Land with your hands out. Dive and gradually lower the remainder of your body as you duck your head and roll forward in a tucked position. Come to a stand.

Common Errors:

(1) Failing to do an extended handstand before starting the forward roll. (2) Having poor arm throw on the full twist. (3) Diving out and not up.

Coaching Points:

(1) Complete the handstand before you do the forward roll. (2) Be sure your body weight is over your feet before jumping for the full twist. (3) Dive up.

Practice Hints:

(1) Use several mats in the first attempts. (2) Be sure your body is on balance when you come out of the full twist before attempting the dive roll. (3) Use your arms as a shock absorber to protect your neck in the dive roll. (4) Make sure that your hips are over your head as you come down in the dive roll.

Spotting Tips:

As you kick your legs to the handstand, the spotter catches them and lifts up. He holds your legs until the roll is on your back, then he releases you. He moves forward during the full twist and cradles your hips in his arms as you go into the dive. He lowers your body in a rolled position.

28. Handstand Forward Straight Leg Roll

Begin from a track start with your fingers pointing straight ahead. Keep your arms straight and your head up as you kick up first one leg, then the other. Be sure your body passes through a good stretched handstand. Start the forward, downward motion of the roll by allowing your feet to go beyond the vertical. Bend your arms and duck your head, rolling down on the back of your neck and shoulders. Be sure your legs are together and straight. Place your hands outside your knees. Push up and back as your head and chest snap forward, adding body momentum to overcome the large base made by the straight legs. Come up to a standing position.

Common Errors:

(1) Failing to reach the extended handstand position before starting the forward roll. (2) Dropping from the handstand to the forward roll, landing directly on your back and shoulders. (3) Bending your legs as you come out of the forward roll.

Coaching Points:

(1) Roll down from the handstand very rapidly. (2) Keep a tight pike coming up into the straight leg roll. (3) Push with your arms and hands as your body mass moves forward to a stand.

Practice Hints:

(1) Do the handstand on a stack of mats and allow your feet to drop when coming out of the forward straight leg roll. Use a downhill mat pattern to help you establish momentum. (2) Work on flexibility by sitting on a mat with your legs straight and together, then bend forward from the waist and tuck your toes.

Spotting Tips:

As you kick into a handstand, the spotter grasps your legs to assist you as they come to a vertical position over your hands. He checks the handstand and stretches your body if it is sagging. He holds your legs until you duck your head and bend your arms, coming into the forward roll. He then releases you, steps behind, and aids you in coming to a standing position.

29. Combination Back Roll Jump with Half Twist, Dive Forward Roll, Handstand Forward Roll with Straight Legs

Begin from a standing position with your back to the mat. Sit back and place your hands by your side to help lower yourself. Tuck your head to your chest and round your shoulders and back when going into the back roll. As soon as your feet leave the mat, roll back, place your hands by your head, and lift up as your body weight passes over your head in the roll. Coming up on your feet, jump with a half twist by extending your legs and lifting up your arms obliquely. Look in the direction which you are twisting. Dive up by swinging your arms back and up. Keep your head in line with your body and allow it to pike. Use your hands coming out of the dive into the roll, letting your head and shoulders down gently. Come out of the dive roll in a tucked position. Lean forward and place your hands down eight inches in front of your feet. Keep your arms straight and your head up as you kick into the handstand. Extend your body as you reach the vertical position. Allow your legs to initiate the forward motion into the roll by passing beyond the vertical. Bend your arms and tuck your head as you come down into the forward roll. Keep your legs straight and together when coming up. Place your hands beside your knees, pushing up and back. Snap the top part of your trunk forward, adding to the body momentum being built up.

Common Errors:

(1) Failing to push with your hands as your body weight passes over your head in the back roll. (2) Diving out, not up. (3) Beginning the forward roll before reaching the handstand. (4) Not keeping your legs straight when coming out of the straight leg roll.

Coaching Points:

(1) When your head rolls under in the back roll, lift your hips and push with your arms. (2) Take your dive up, not out. (3) Extend your body in the handstand. (4) Flex your thigh muscles as you come up in the straight leg forward roll.

Practice Hints:

(1) Review the back roll. (2) Use a stick and dive over it to gain height in the dive roll. (3) On a stack of mats, practice the handstand forward straight leg roll down-hill.

Spotting Tips:

The spotter lifts your hips as your head passes under your body on the back roll. He then turns and cradles your body in the dive roll. He moves forward and catches your legs as you kick into the handstand.

ACROBATICS

These skills require flexibility in the back, leg, and shoulder regions. Basic acrobatics involve no free flight. At all times the hands or feet are in contact with the mat. Mastery of the mechanics of aerial movement is essential in all acrobatic work.

30. Cartwheel

Start from a side position facing the mat. Lean forward from your front leg, shifting your body weight to the side and forward placing your first hand (the one that is along your body and pointed toward the mat) down 12 inches from your front foot. Thrust your back leg vigorously up and over your head, causing body rotation. Reach out with your second hand (the one which is raised to a vertical position above your head) putting it down 12 inches from your first hand. Just before it touches the mat, your bent first leg extends, driving your body up and adding to the rotation. Show flexibility in the split. Land on your first leg 12 inches from your second hand. Put your last leg 12 inches from the first one. Do the cartwheel in four evenly spaced counts, with your arms and legs forming spokes of a wheel.

Common Errors:

(1) Failing to take a side position as you begin the cartwheel. (2) Having inadequate markings of the one, two hand placement. (3) Having insignificant spread of your legs over your head when in the cartwheel.

Coaching Points:

(1) Be sure the cartwheel is done from the side. (2) Reach down for the placement of your second hand. (3) Throw the thrust leg over your head. (4) Be sure to extend the drive leg as you push.

Practice Hints:

(1) From a standing position, practice thrusting the throw leg

Cartwheel

and extending the drive leg. (2) Do the whole movement to the count of four.

Spotting Tips:

As you bend to the side and start to place your first hand down, the spotter places his hand nearest you around your waist. As you reach the straddle handstand position, his other hand goes around your waist to give you direction and to lift you up.

31. Round-off

Start from a standing position facing the mat with both arms above your head. Bend forward at your waist and flex one knee, placing your hands about 14 inches from your first foot. Your first hand goes in front of your body while your second hand reaches around behind your first one. Thrust your leg up to a vertical position. As your legs reach the vertical, make a half turn. Snap your legs down forcefully, push with your arms, and shrug your shoulders, pushing the top of your body up as your legs come down. Stand and face the same direction from which you started.

Common Errors:

(1) Failing to place your hands in front of your body at the beginning of the round-off. (2) Not reaching the handstand position with your legs before the half turn. (3) As your legs snap down, failing to bring your arms and shoulders up.

Coaching Points:

(1) Place your first hand down directly in front of you. (2) Be sure your second hand goes behind and to the side of your first one. (3) Be sure that the round-off passes through a vertical plane.

Practice Hints:

(1) When you are learning the round-off, do it from a stand. (2) Learn the skill slowly and try to interpret the various phases of it. (3) Draw a line down the mat from which to start and finish.

Spotting Tips:

As you place your hands down and kick up to the handstand, the spotter grasps your legs and assists you with the half turn. He releases you as you snap down.

36

32. Back Bend

From a prone position on the mats, place your hands beside your head with your fingers pointing toward your feet. Place your feet next to your seat, bending your knees. Slowly bridge your body up by bending back and pushing up with your arms and legs. Drop your head back. Gradually extend the back bend to your maximum potential. Gently lower your body to the mat.

Common Errors:

(1) Placing your feet and hands too wide. (2) Doing the bend from your hips rather than your back. (3) Bending too much on the first try.

Coaching Points:

(1) Do the first few back bends slowly to loosen your back muscles. (2) Place your hands in close to your head and be sure your feet are next to your seat before you attempt to bridge up. (3) Lower your body gently when coming out of the backbend.

Spotting Tips:

As you begin to extend your legs and arms, the spotter places one hand under your shoulders and reaches across your body, placing his other hand under your hips. He also lifts your body as you bridge it up.

33. Handstand Front Limber

From a standing position facing the mat, bend forward from your waist, placing both hands about 14 inches from your feet. Keep your arms straight and your head up as you kick up to the handstand. As you reach the handstand, let your feet go beyond it. Come down to your feet as you arch your back to form a body bridge. Push with your arms and move your hips forward as you lift your upper trunk to a standing position.

Common Errors:

(1) Bending your back too soon before your feet and hips are over your hands. (2) Flexing at your hips rather than in the small of your back. (3) Not pushing up enough with your arms when coming to a stand.

Coaching Points:

(1) Do the back bend from your back, not your hips. (2) Allow your hips to move forward coming up from the back bridge to the stand. (3) Follow your head with your arms and extend them behind it.

Practice Hints:

(1) Do the handstand on a stack of mats and let your feet land on the lower level when coming up. (2) Be sure you warm your back up

Handstand Front Limber

before doing the front limber. (3) Work on the handstand limber with a spotter to help you get the feeling of the movement.

Spotting Tips:

The spotter stands near your side in front of you. As you kick into the handstand, he grasps your legs just above your thighs. As you go beyond the handstand, he lets his hands slide down so that one of his arms is under your hips while the other is under your shoulder. He assists you in coming up from the bridge position to a standing one.

34. Front Walkover

From a standing position facing the mat, raise either leg up as high as possible and lift your arms to a vertical position above your head. Step forward on your leg which you lifted and place your hands about 14 inches in front of your foot. Keep your arms straight and your

Front Walkover

head up as you kick your back leg up and over. Extend the drive leg up. Pass momentarily through a straddle handstand as your legs continue over your hands. Bend your back bringing the thrust leg down on the mat first. Push up and forward with your arms as you bring the drive leg down 18 inches from your first one. Follow your upper body with your arms extended behind your head as the top of your trunk and head come to a standing position. Do the walkover in three counts.

Common Errors:

(1) Failing to present yourself as described in the first sentence above. (2) Placing your hands too close to your feet. (3) Bending too soon before your hips are over the base.

Coaching Points:

(1) Present yourself before placing your hands down at the beginning of the skill. (2) Do not begin the back bend until your hips are in line with your hands. (3) Watch for proper arm patterns when coming out of the walkover.

Practice Hints:

(1) Practice the handstand, back bend, and completion. (2) Do the walkover on a stack of mats, allowing your feet to land on the lower mat. (3) Concentrate on keeping your weight forward when coming out of the walkover.

Spotting Tips:

As you place your hands down, the spotter places one hand on the small of your back and the other one on your shoulder. He assists you when you come out of the walkover.

35. Backover

Begin with your back to the mat, your feet six inches apart, and your arms stretched above your head. Slowly bend back by stretching your neck and looking down the mat. Bend your back as you move your body down. Place your hands first on the mat about two feet from your feet. As you do the handstand on the mat, use your fingers and head to continue the motion by splitting your legs and by bringing one leg over and then the other. Push the mat with your fingers and raise your head as one leg reaches the vertical to help bring the other one over. Show as wide a leg split as possible. Land in a standing position.

Common Errors:

(1) Not stretching your arms enough above your head as you start the back bend. (2) Doing the first part of the bend with your hips and knees rather than your back. (3) Not using your fingers and lifting your head to aid in pushing your legs up over your head.

Coaching Points:

(1) Be sure your arms are above your head as you begin the back bend. (2) Be sure the back bend originates in your back, not at your hips and knees. (3) Show as much flexibility as possible in the straddle leg position. (4) Use your arms and head to aid your body in rotation when going over.

Practice Hints:

(1) Use a spotter and have him lift your hips as you go over. (2) Bridge up into the back bend and kick over. (3) For protection use a low side horse or mat to kick over.

Spotting Tips:

As you start into the back bend, the spotter cradles your upper back in his arms to lower you to a back-bend position. Then he moves one arm between your hips and knees and pushes up on your legs and hips to help you go over the top.

36. Back Walkover

Do this skill with three spokes, using three even counts in the puppet string method pretending you have a single string attached to your first foot, your hands, and your head. As you move one, you must move all three. Start with your back to the mat facing out with the leg that you wish to raise first slightly in front of the other. Place your arms obliquely and forward. Raise your leg and lift your head up and back until your hands touch the mat with your first leg in a vertical position. Push off with your other one. Press with your fingers and raise your head to add to the rotation of your body over your hands. Be as flexible as possible in the leg split and try to make the three even counts coming over.

Common Errors:

(1) Doing a back bend and then kicking your split legs over. (2) Not using your arms and head to aid in body rotation. (3) Having improper distance between your legs and arms in the three spokes.

Coaching Points:

(1) Be sure to use the puppet string method. (2) Mark a three-count movement. (3) Show as much flexibility as possible in your split legs as they go over the base. (4) Tighten your thigh muscles to help keep your legs straight on the walkover.

Practice Hints:

(1) Look in the mirror to practice the puppet string action of your first leg, arms, and head. (2) Have the spotter lift your first leg up toward your chest, helping to stretch your legs and to push them apart in the split handstand.

Back Walkover

Spotting Tips:

The spotter places one hand behind your shoulders while his other one grasps your lifted leg. As you bend your back, he supports your upper back with one hand and lifts up and back on your other leg.

37. Front Tinsica

Do this skill in an even marked four count, two for your hands, two for your feet. Begin by standing to the side of the mat. Have one arm by your side and the other by your head reaching vertically. Using a side bend, place your first hand down with your fingers facing the side of the mat. Thrust the throw leg over your head as you reach out for the placement of your second hand. As your second hand goes down, execute a quarter turn of your hips before your first leg touches the mat, causing your body to do a side bend. Bring your legs out in a walkout fashion.

Common Errors:

(1) Facing forward rather than sideward on the cartwheel. (2) Doing a half turn with your hips instead of a quarter turn. (3) Failing to mark the four count of your hands and feet.

Coaching Points:

(1) Remember to start from the side. (2) Watch your hand placement to be sure the hands are in line. (3) Execute only a quarter turn with your hips. Bring your back up with a side bend, not a back bend.

Practice Hints:

(1) Put a line on the mat and be sure your hands touch the line and are straight. (2) Have the spotter touch your hips as your second hand touches the mat. (3) Be sure to look forward coming out of the tinsica, helping to do the quarter turn of your body.

Spotting Tips:

As your first hand goes down, the spotter supports you around your waist. When your second hand touches the mat, his other hand grasps your waist to help you execute a quarter turn. He follows you to a standing position.

Front Tinsica

38. Combination Front Roll Walkout, Cartwheel, Back Roll Tuck

From a standing position facing the mat, bend forward at your waist placing your hands on the mat eight inches in front of your feet. Tuck your chin to your chest and round your shoulders and back as you extend your legs going into a forward roll. Halfway through the roll, tuck one leg in close to your seat and extend the other. Come out of the forward roll into a walkout position. Bring your body weight up to a standing position, one leg ahead of the other. Bend forward and place your first hand down on the cartwheel as your thrust your throw leg up. Reach out to place your second hand in line with the drive foot and your first hand. After your second hand goes down, finish extending the drive leg and bring it up and over. Come out of the cartwheel and make a quarter turn facing in the direction from which you came. Sit back going into the back roll. Tuck your chin on your chest and round your shoulders and back as you fall back. Place your hands beside your head as your feet leave the mat going up and back. As your body weight passes over your head, push with your arms taking the weight off your neck. Bring your feet over and land in a standing position.

Common Errors:

(1) Failing to tuck your chin on your chest and round your back. (2) Lacking complete extension of the straight leg in the walkout. (3) Placing your hands simultaneously rather than marking a one, two count. (4) Having poor hand placement by your head as you do the back roll.

Coaching Points:

(1) Use your arms to lower your body for the forward roll. (2) Be sure that the walkout position is on the same side as the cartwheel. (3) Place your hands and feet in a straight line. (4) After the cartwheel, shift your weight back before going into the back roll. (5) Place your hands beside your head as you go into the back roll.

Practice Hints:

(1) Review the sequence of the skills involved in the forward roll. (2) Practice the last half of the forward roll walkout. (3) Coordinate the mechanics of the throw leg and drive leg in executing the cartwheel. (4) Do a back roll several times by taking two steps back and squatting down into the roll.

Spotting Tips:

The spotter moves along the mat with his knees bent, ready to move and assist when necessary.

39. Combination Back Roll Extension Stepout, Cartwheel

Stand with your back to the mat. Sit back by bending forward at your waist and sitting back at your hips. Place your hands beside your hips as you fall back. As soon as your seat touches the mat, put your hands beside your head. Tuck your legs as they begin going back. When your hands touch the mat beside your head, shoot your legs up to a vertical position and extend your arms, lifting your head up when going into a handstand. Split your legs by putting one leg back and the other one forward. Come down on the leg that went back. As you come to a stand, make a half turn and step forward on the other one. Continue this motion by reaching out and placing your first hand down on the cartwheel while extending the throw leg up and over, placing the second hand in line with your feet 12 inches from the first one. Extend your drive leg, pushing it up and over your hands. Come to a standing position.

Common Errors:

(1) Sitting down too hard out of the stand. (2) Not placing your hands beside your head in the back roll. (3) Shooting your leg back, not up to a vertical position. (4) Placing your hands together in the cartwheel.

Coaching Points:

(1) Bend forward at your waist before you sit back going into the roll. (2) Shoot your feet to a vertical in the roll extension. (3) Do a half turn before going into the cartwheel. (4) Place your hands and feet in line during the cartwheel. (5) Do a four count in the cartwheel.

Practice Hints:

(1) Have the spotter lift your legs as you shoot to the handstand. (2) Kick up to a handstand, split your legs, and practice stepping out as you come down into the cartwheel. Put your hands and feet on a line as you do the cartwheel.

Spotting Tips:

As you roll back and place your hands on the mat, the spotter grasps your legs as you shoot them up to the vertical. He then lifts your hips, steadies you as you split your legs, and lets his hands slide down to your waist to assist you as you lower yourself. He then catches you just above your waist and helps you throw your leg over, following you until both legs come down out of the cartwheel to a stand.

40. Back Tinsica

Do this skill in four counts, two for your arms and two for your legs. Stand with your back to the mat. As you bend back raise your right leg, if the right leg is to be the first one over, while you reach up and back with your left arm. Bring your second hand down as your first leg passes the vertical position. Push off with your second leg to complete the four spokes of the tinsica. Place your hands and feet in a straight line.

Common Errors:

(1) Placing both hands down at the same time rather than one at a time. (2) Having poor direction as your feet pass over your hands. (3) Having an incomplete four count through the tinsica.

Coaching Points:

(1) Be sure to use your opposite arm and leg going into the tinsica. (2) Place your hands and feet in a straight line. (3) Be sure your feet and legs travel through a frontal plane as they go over the top.

Practice Hints:

(1) Practice lifting your opposite arm and leg in preparation for the back tinsica. (2) Chalk your hands so that as you do the tinsica you will see whether your hand placement is correct. (3) Do several back bends and walkovers as warm-ups before attempting the back tinsica.

Spotting Tips:

As you raise your first leg, bend back and place your hand down, as the spotter places one hand under your shoulders. As your second hand goes down, he lifts your first leg up and back to assist you in direction. He follows the movement of your body until your first foot lands on the mat.

41. Front Limber, Front Roll Walkout, Cartwheel

Start from a standing position facing the mat. Bend forward at your waist and bend your knees placing your hands 14 inches in front of your feet. Keep your arms straight and your head up as you kick your legs up into a handstand. Allow your feet to continue beyond the vertical, coming down as you bend your back to bridge it up. Bring your hands up off the mat. Come up to a standing position. Bend forward at your waist as you bend your legs, placing your hands in front of your feet and under your shoulders. Tuck your chin to your chest and round your shoulders and back. Push with your legs and roll forward using your arms to protect your head as your body weight comes over. Straighten one leg while you tuck the other one. Keep your head forward. Come up to a standing position with one leg ahead of the other. Reach forward and down, placing your first hand down for the cartwheel. Extend the thrust leg up and over as you reach forward and out for your second hand. Extend the drive leg as it goes over your head. Push off with your second arm as you come up to a standing position.

Common Errors:

(1) Bending your back too soon before your hips are over your hands. (2) Bringing your hands and upper body up as soon as your feet come down. (3) Rounding your back improperly for the forward roll. (4) Failing to extend your first leg in the walkout of the forward roll. (5) Not marking your hand placement properly.

Coaching Points:

(1) Do your back bend in the front limber after you have reached the handstand position. (2) Keep your arms extended and close to your ears as you come out of the back bend. (3) Get your body weight forward before you attempt to go into the forward roll. (4) Tighten your thigh muscles on your straight leg coming to the walkout position. (5) Reach out for hand placement on the cartwheel.

Practice Hints:

(1) Practice the front limber on a stack of mats. (2) Stand and bend back slightly, then return to a stand with your arms straight behind your head and your elbows close to your ears. (3) From a sitting position, roll back to your shoulders and practice coming to a walkout position. (4) Use lines on the mats to help with the placement and direction of your hands and feet.

Spotting Tips:

As you go into a handstand, the spotter grasps your legs and assists you in this skill. His hands move from your legs to the small of your back and shoulders to assist you in the bridge position. He helps you to a stand, moves forward as you do the forward roll. When you come out of the forward roll walkout, he places one hand on your midsection and, when you kick up, his second hand goes around your other side at your waist, aiding you in going into the cartwheel.

42. Combination Front Limber, Front Roll Jump with Half Twist, Backover

Start from a standing position facing the mat. Bend forward at your waist and knees, placing your hands down about 14 inches in front of your first foot. Kick your legs up to a vertical postion. Allow them to go beyond the vertical and come down, bridging your back up with your hands and feet. Allow your arms to follow the top of your body up as your feet make contact with the mat. Straighten your arms behind your head and close to your ears. Allow your body weight to move forward after standing out of a front limber. Place your hands down in front of your knees. Use your arms to help protect your neck as your body weight passes over. Extend your legs as you tuck your head and round your shoulders going into a forward roll. Allow your body weight to come over your feet. Extend your legs and swing your arms up obliquely to a vertical, making a half twist of your body. Upon landing with both feet together, place your arms above your head and bend your body back as you look back with your head, bending your back until you place your hands on the mat. Press the mat with your finger tips and raise your head as you shove up and over with your feet. Finish the skill in a standing position.

Common Errors:

(1) Starting the back bend before your hips are over your hands. (2) Recovering from the front limber with your arms to your side rather than beside your ears above your head. (3) Improper rounding of your neck and shoulders going into the forward roll. (4) Jumping with the twist too soon. (5) Bending your back at your hips instead of your back.

Coaching Points:

(1) Keep your arms straight and your head up when kicking into a handstand. (2) Be sure you do the back bend after your feet have passed the vertical position. (3) Make the movement in the forward roll fluent to add enough momentum for the jump with a half turn. (4) Be on balance before you attempt to go into the backover. (5) Use your hands and head in rotating in the backover.

Practice Hints:

(1) Do a front limber on a stack of mats and land on the lower mat. (2) Practice squeezing your ears with your arms when coming out of the front limber. (3) Practice the mechanics of the jump with a half turn. (4) Practice the arm throw pattern while jumping in front of a mirror. (5) Do a back bend over a stack of mats or a low side horse.

Spotting Tips:

As you kick into a handstand, the spotter grasps your legs to help you extend your body. When your feet pass beyond the handstand, his hands move to the small of your back and shoulders to assist you in the back bend and to aid you as you come out of it. He then moves forward to your side. As you come out of the forward roll, he steps behind and places his hand on your waist, pushing to help you turn. He again moves to your side to assist you as you do the back bend by placing one hand under your shoulders and his other under the small of your back to aid you as you finish the combination.

43. Front Walkover, Cartwheel, Back Walkover

Start from a standing position facing the mat. Bend forward and place both hands on it a few inches in front of your shoulders. Keep your arms straight and your head up. Kick the throw leg up and over. As the throw leg reaches the vertical position, extend the drive leg, bringing it up and over off the mat, adding to the forward momentum coming out of the front walkover. Bring your second leg down 16 inches in front of your first one. Straighten your arms behind your head and close to your ears. Keep your body weight moving forward. As you make a quarter turn, place your first hand down 14 inches from your foot and throw the thrust leg up and over. Place your second hand down 14 inches from your first one as you extend the drive leg up and over. Place your hands and feet in a straight line in a four count action. Come to a straddle standing position. Execute a quarter turn back and raise your first leg and arm up as you begin bending your back. Use the puppet string method of moving your head, arms, and legs. Put your hands straight behind your head and shoulder-width apart on the mat as your first leg begins its flight up and nears the vertical. Press with your finger tips and raise your head to add to the body momentum as you push off the mat with your second leg carrying it up and over. Bring your first foot down as your hands come up off the mat. Raise your chest and upper body as you keep your second leg extended from your trunk.

Common Errors:

(1) Starting the back bend of the front walkover with your hips in a vertical position. (2) Failing to show the proper arm position coming out of the front walkover. (3) Not completing the quarter turn before going into the cartwheel. (4) Having an inadequate four count of your hands and feet during the cartwheel. (5) Doing the quarter turn too soon for the back bend before your body weight is over your back foot. (6) Not raising your first leg as your head and arms go back for the back bend. (7) Failing to use your hands and head to give your body momentum when going over in the back walkover.

Coaching Points:

(1) Keep a straight back in the front walkover until your hips are over the base and then bend for the walkout. (2) Keep your arms extended behind your head and close to your ears. (3) Make a quarter turn before going into the cartwheel after the front walkover. (4) Keep your hands and feet in a straight line. (5) Raise your first leg along with your arms while your head goes back into a back bend for the back walkover. (6) Maintain a correct body line coming out of the back walkover.

Practice Hints:

(1) Master each of the skills in the series before you attempt to put them together. (2) Do a front walkover on a stack of mats to a regular mat, then do a cartwheel. (3) Practice the walkover making a quarter turn, then the cartwheel making a quarter turn into the back walkover.

Spotting Tips:

As you go into a front walkover, the spotter places one hand in the small of your back and the other on your shoulder as you come out of the front walkover. As you go into a cartwheel, he places one hand in your mid-section. As your first leg goes over your head, his second hand grasps your waist and helps you go into the cartwheel. He puts his hand in the small of your back as you do the back bend going into the back walkover.

44. Combination Back Walkover with Half Turn, Front Walkover

Start with your back to the mat. Use the puppet string method going into a back walkover by first raising your leg and arms while putting your head back as you begin the back bend. As you place your hands on the mat, your first leg goes up and over. Press your fingers into the mat and raise your head up for momentum. Push off the mat with your second leg, bringing it up and over. Keep your second leg extended on the back walkover and push off the mat with your arms and shoulders. As you come up, show a correct body line. After the first foot lands and before the second one comes down, execute a half turn. Step forward and place your hands down just in front of your shoulders. Keep your arms straight and your head up as you kick your first leg up and over. Do not let your back bend until your hips have come to a vertical line over your hands. As your first leg passes the vertical position, push off with your second one bringing it up and over. Use your arms and shoulders to push the upper body upward as you walk out of the front walkover. Extend your arms behind your head with your elbows close to your ears.

Common Errors:

(1) Not using the puppet string method. (2) Having improper body line coming out of the walkover. (3) Making your half turn going into the front walkover after your second foot touches the mat. (4) Placing your hands too close to your feet going into the front walkover. (5) Having your arm positions coming out of the walkover to the side rather than behind your head.

Coaching Points:

(1) Looking in a mirror, practice the first phase of the puppet string method with your leg, arms, and head. (2) Remember that the back walkover is done in three counts. (3) Do a half turn before your second foot comes down out of the back walkover. (4) Place your hands slightly in front of your shoulders as you go into the front walkover. (5) Keep your arms straight, as they follow your head and your upper trunk as you come out of the front walkover.

Practice Hints:

(1) Warm up well with slow back bends before attempting a walkover. (2) Remember the puppet string action and raise your leg and

arms while putting your head back at the same time. (3) From a standing position, practice making a half turn as if you were coming out
of the back walkover to go into the front walkover. Be sure the half
turn is done before your second foot touches the mat.

Spotting Tips:

As you begin to raise your leg and arms while putting your head
back, the spotter places one hand in the small of your back, assisting
as you go into the back bend. His other hand lifts your first leg and
helps in its rotation by pushing it over. He moves forward. As you
place your hands down and kick your leg up, he places one hand in
the small of your back and the other on your shoulder, aiding you as
you come up.

45. Combination Back Walkover Quarter Turn, Cartwheel Quarter Turn, Front Walkover

Start with your back to the mat. Use the puppet string method to
go into the back walkover by raising your first leg and your arms, while
putting your head back as you begin the back bend. As you place your
hands on the mat, bring your first leg up and over. Press your fingers
into the mat and raise your head up to add momentum. Push off the
mat with your second leg bringing it up and over. Keep it extended on
the back walkover and push off the mat with your arms and shoulders.
As you come up, show a correct body line. After your first foot lands
and before the second one comes down, do a quarter turn. Keep your
body weight moving forward as you place your first hand down 14
inches from your foot. Throw the thrust leg up and over. Put your
second hand down 14 inches from your first one as you extend the
drive leg up and over. Place your hands and feet in four counts on a
straight line. After your first foot comes down and before the second
one lands, do a quarter turn. Step forward and place your hands down
just in front of your shoulders. Keep your arms straight and your head
up as you kick your first leg up and over. Do not let your back bend
until your hips have come to a vertical line over your hands. As your
first leg passes the vertical position, push off with your second one
bringing it up and over. Use your arms and shoulders to push your
upper body up as you walk out of the front walkover. Extend your
arms behind your head with your elbows close to your ears.

Common Errors:

(1) Not using the puppet string method in lifting your leg and
arms, and in putting your head back. (2) Not pressing your hands and
raising your head when your body is upside down in the back walkover. (3) Making the quarter turn too late after the second foot is on

the mat. (4) Placing your arms too close to your feet as you kick into the cartwheel. (5) Doing the back bend before your hips reach the vertical position above the base in the front walkover.

Coaching Points:

(1) Practice the puppet string method of your leg, arms, and head from a standing position without doing a complete back bend. (2) Use your arms and head to keep the body momentum going over in a walkover. (3) Do a quarter turn while your second leg is still in the air. (4) Mark a four count with your feet and hands on the placement of the cartwheel. (5) Make a quarter turn on one foot. (6) Place your hands in front of your shoulders going into the front walkover. (7) Use your arms and head as you come out of the front walkover.

Practice Hints:

(1) Warm up before attempting this skill. (2) From a standing position, do the puppet string movement in a mirror, checking to be sure it is correct. (3) From a standing position, practice making a quarter turn for a cartwheel and a front walkover. (4) Use the spotter to assist you at the small of your back coming out of the back and front walkover.

Spotting Tips:

As you raise your leg and arms while your head goes back, the spotter places one hand on the small of your back and his other grasps your first leg and assists by pushing it over. He then moves forward. As you place your first hand down on the cartwheel, he places one hand on your rib cage. As your first leg passes the vertical, his second hand grasps your waist and assists you in rotation and direction when going over.

46. Combination Front Tinsica, Cartwheel, Back Walkover with Half Turn, Front Walkover

Mark this skill with four counts, two with your hands and two with your feet. Begin by standing on the side of the mat. Have one arm down by your side and the other one by your head reaching to the vertical. Using a side bend, place your first hand down with your fingers facing the side of the mat. Thrust the throw leg over your head as you reach out for the placement of your second hand. As your second hand goes down, execute a quarter turn of your hips before your first leg touches the mat, causing your body to do a side bend. Bring your legs out in a walkout fashion. Keep your body weight moving forward as you place your first hand down 14 inches from your first foot while you throw the thrust leg up and over. Bring your second hand down 14 inches from the first one as you extend the drive leg up and over. Place your hands and feet in a straight line with a four count action. After your first foot lands and before the second one comes down, do a quarter turn. Use the puppet string method going into the back walkover by raising your first leg, your arms, and by putting your head back as you begin the back bend. As you place your hands on the mat, bring your first leg up and over. Press your fingers into the mat and raise your head up, adding to the momentum. Push off the mat with your second leg, bringing it up and over. On the back walkover keep your second leg extended and push off the mat with your arms and shoulders. As you come up, show a correct body line. After your first foot lands and before the second one comes down, do a half turn. Step forward and place your hands down just in front of your shoulders. Keep your arms straight and your head up as you kick your first leg up and over. Do not let your back bend until your hips have come to a vertical line over your hands. As your first leg passes the vertical position, push off the mat with your second one driving it up and over. Use your arms and shoulders to push your upper body as you walk out of the front walkover. Extend your arms behind your head with your elbows close to your ears.

Common Errors:

(1) Placing your hands in line without a one, two count. (2) Not doing a quarter turn as you come out of the tinsica. (3) Placing your first hand down in the cartwheel too close to your first foot. (4) Not having your arms above your head as you go into the back bend for the back walkover. (5) Doing a half turn too soon. (6) Bending your back before your hips reach a vertical position.

Coaching Points:

(1) Place your hands and feet in a straight line. (2) Use a side bend rather than a back bend when coming out of the tinsica. (3) Remember the cartwheel is a side skill. (4) Mark a four count in doing the cartwheel. (5) Be sure your body is in the right position before doing a quarter turn for the back walkover. (6) Get your arms up behind your head before going into the back bend for the back walkover. (7) Do a half twist before your second leg comes down on the mat going into a front walkover. (8) Place your hands slightly ahead of your shoulders going into the front walkover. (9) Make your back bend when your hips are in the vertical position above the base.

Practice Hints:

(1) Draw a line on the mat to check the placement of your hands and feet. (2) Practice doing a side bend from a standing position, learning how the position feels. (3) Use a line on the mat for the cartwheel for your hand and foot placement. (4) From a standing position practice the markings of the cartwheel by throwing the throw leg and extending the drive leg. (5) Use the puppet string method on the back walkover when you raise your leg and arms and when you put your

head back. (6) Show as much flexibility as possible on the back and front walkover.

Spotting Tips:

As you begin the tinsica, the spotter places one hand in your midsection as your first hand goes down. His other hand goes around your waist as you place your second hand down. He moves along with the series, doing the same thing with the cartwheel that he did with the tinsica. As you go into the back walkover, he places his hands on the small of your back as you lower yourself for the back bend. He then places one hand on your shoulder and his other one on the small of your back as you go into the back walkover.

47. Combination Front Walkover, Cartwheel, Back Tinsica

Step forward, raising your arms to a position in front of your shoulders. Keep your arms straight and your head up as you kick up and over. Do not let your back bend until your hips have come to a vertical line over your hands. As your first leg passes the vertical position, push off with the second one letting it come up and over. Use your arms and shoulders to push your upper body up as you walk out of the front walkover. Extend your arms behind your head with your elbows close to your ears. After your first hand lands and before the second one comes down, do a quarter turn. Keep your body weight moving forward as you place your first hand down 14 inches from your foot. Throw the thrust leg up and over. Bring your second hand down 14 inches from the first one as you extend the drive leg up and over. Place your hands and feet in a straight line in a four count action. After your first foot lands and before your second one comes down, do a quarter turn. Show the four spokes of the tinsica in this skill. Begin by standing with your back to the mat. As you bend back, raise your right leg if your right leg is to be the first one over, bringing your left arm up and back reaching for the mat. Place your second hand down as your first leg passes the vertical position. Push off the mat with your second leg, completing the four spokes. Place your hands and feet in a straight line.

Common Errors:

(1) Placing your hands too close to your forward foot going into the walkover. (2) Starting your back bend in the front walkover too soon. (3) Not having your hands in line on the cartwheel. (4) Placing your hands down at the same time on the back tinsica rather than a one, two count. (5) Having a poor body line coming out of the tinsica.

Coaching Points:

(1) Place your hands down and slightly in front of your shoulders. (2) Do a back bend after your hips reach the vertical position. (3)

Reach out while marking a one, two count of your hands in the cartwheel. (4) Show flexibility in the leg split position on all three skills. (5) Use the puppet string method on your leg, your arm lift, and your head placement on the back tinsica.

Practice Hints:

(1) Do a front walkover on a stack of mats, allowing your feet to land on the lower mat when coming out of it going into the cartwheel. (2) Concentrate on getting your weight forward as you come out of the walkover when going into the cartwheel. (3) From a standing position, practice the throw pattern of the thrust leg and the extension of the drive leg in the cartwheel. (4) Make four counts for the cartwheel as you do it. (5) Practice lifting your opposite arm and leg in preparation of the back tinsica. (6) Use chalk on your hands to mark your hand placement.

Spotting Tips:

As you begin the walkover by placing your hands down, the spotter places one hand on the small of your back. As you kick your throw leg up and over, his second hand touches your throw leg and assists in turning you. He follows the front walkover until its completion. As you go into the cartwheel, his first hand goes to your mid-section when you place your first hand down. As you thrust the throw leg, his second hand goes around your waist, aiding you by lifting your hips and in rotating you. His first hand stays on your hand, and then moves to the small of your back. As you go into the back bend, he keeps one hand in the small of your back and places his second hand on your throw leg to help you rotate and give you good direction.

48. Combination Back Tinsica, Cartwheel

Do this in four counts, showing the use of the four spokes which are your arms and legs. Begin by standing with your back to the mat. As you bend backward, raise your right leg, if your right leg is to be the first one over, and lift your left arm up and back, reaching for the mat. Place your second hand down as your first leg passes the vertical position and your second leg pushes off the mat, completing the four spokes of the tinsica. Place your hands and feet in a straight line. After your first foot lands and before the second one comes down, do a quarter turn. Keep your body weight moving forward as you place your first hand down and over. Put your second hand down 14 inches from the first one as you extend the drive leg up and over. Place your hands and feet in a four count action in a straight line. Come out in a straddle standing position.

Common Errors:

(1) Placing both hands down on the mat at the same time rather than a one, two count. (2) Having poor direction as your feet pass over

your hands. (3) Failing to show the side position as you go into the cartwheel. (4) Having inadequate marking of the one, two hand placement. (5) Having an insufficient spread of your legs over your head in the cartwheel.

Coaching Points:

(1) Be sure to use your opposite arm and leg when going into the back bend of the tinsica. (2) Place your hands and feet in a straight line. (3) Have your feet and legs pass directly through the frontal plane as they go over the top. (4) Be sure the cartwheel is done from the side position. (5) Reach for the placement of your second hand in the cartwheel. (6) Use the proper mechanics on the throw and thrust legs.

Practice Hints:

(1) Practice lifting your opposite arm and leg doing the puppet string method for the tinsica. (2) Chalk your hands before doing a tinsica and afterward check for the proper hand placement. (3) From a standing position, practice the thrust of the throw leg and the extension of the drive leg for the cartwheel. (4) Count four counts for your hands and feet on the cartwheel.

Spotting Tips:

As you raise your leg and arms going into the back bend, the spotter places one hand in the small of your back and his other assists your first leg as it goes over your head in the tinsica. As you begin the cartwheel, he places one hand in your mid-section and the other grasps your waist as your second leg leaves the mat.

49. One-Arm Cartwheel with First Arm Down

Begin from a side position facing outward. Bend sideways, placing your first hand down 14 inches from the drive leg. Thrust the throw leg up and over as you extend the drive leg by pushing off the mat going up and over. Push off with your arm down and raise your head as your first leg comes down and your second leg stretches toward the rear and mat.

Common Errors:

(1) Placing your first hand too close to the drive foot. (2) Having poor direction of the throw leg going over the top. (3) Failing to extend your drive leg completely. (4) Having it too close to the other leg as you come out of the cartwheel.

Coaching Points:

(1) Throw the thrust leg as your body bends for the first hand placement. (2) Shove off the mat with your hands and shoulders as your feet pass over your head. (3) Make your hand placement gently.

One-Arm Cartwheel with First Arm Down

Practice Hints:

(1) At first use your second hand on top of your first one. (2) Work the one-arm cartwheel off the stack of mats to the lower mats by placing your hands on the lower mats as your feet kick over.

Spotting Tips:

The spotter stands to the side and in front of you. One of his hands goes in your mid-section as you place your hand down while his other hand goes around your waist as you extend the drive leg. He then lifts your hips and aids you in the direction of the cartwheel.

50. One-Arm Cartwheel, Second Arm Down

Start from a side position facing outward. Bend down and place your second hand down 20 inches from the drive foot. Throw the thrust leg up and over as you extend the drive leg and push off the mat. Allow your legs to rotate over your head and land in a side straddle position one at a time. Push off the mat with your arms and shoulders as your legs start down for the mat.

Common Errors:

(1) Placing your second hand down too close to the drive foot. (2) Failing to thrust the throw leg and extend the drive leg together. (3) Lacking velocity as your legs pass over.

Coaching Points:

(1) Place your second hand 20 inches from the drive foot. (2) Be sure the throw of the thrust leg and the extension of the drive leg are done at the same time. (3) Keep your legs straight as they go over.

Practice Hints:

(1) Use a line on the mat to help you keep the proper direction as your feet and hands touch the mat. (2) From a standing position practice the mechanics of the thrust and extension of the throw and drive leg. (3) Work the cartwheel off a stack of mats, placing your second hand on the lower mats as your feet kick over.

Spotting Tips:

The spotter stands to the side in front of you. As you place your second hand down, he puts one hand in your mid-section. When you thrust the throw leg, his other hand goes on your waist to lift you and aid your direction as your legs and body pass through the frontal plane.

51. Yogi Handstand

Start from a standing position facing the mat. Bend forward and place your hands slightly in front of your shoulders. Tuck your chin

Yogi Handstand

on your chest and look at your toes. Pike your body by letting the hips go forward over your hands with your toes back. Keep your hips forward and your toes back to offset each other and establish balance. As your body weight moves forward, thrust one leg up and down as your other one follows. Push with your arms and shoulders. Raise your head as you come out in a back bend and walkout position.

Common Errors:

(1) Placing your hands too close to the drive foot. (2) Failing to tuck your chin and look at your toes. (3) Not getting your hips far enough over your hands. (4) Collapsing your arms and shoulders as you walk out.

Coaching Points:

(1) Be sure you tuck your head under and look at your toes. (2) Pike your body by putting your hips forward and bending at your waist. (3) Push with your finger tips as your legs open and extend up and down to mat. (4) Keep your arms behind your head as you come up out of the yogi. (Study the illustration of this skill again.)

Practice Hints:

(1) Go into the yogi position against a wall and push off it to return to the mat. (2) Work on a tight pike position while sitting on the floor. (3) Keep your legs straight and together as you bend forward from your waist putting your chest on your knees. (4) At first do not try to hold the yogi, just pass through the position and step out.

Spotting Tips:

As you place your hands down, the spotter places one hand on your shoulder and the other one on your lower back to help you balance while in the yogi handstand. As your body weight moves forward, he steadies your back as you arch and walk out. He follows your motion until you are standing.

52. Combination Cartwheel, One-Arm Cartwheel, Round-Off, Back Roll

Start from a side position on the mat. Place one hand down along your body pointed to the mat and raise the second one to a vertical position above your head. Lean forward off the front leg, shifting your body weight to the side and forward by placing your first hand 12 inches from your front foot. Vigorously thrust the throw leg up and over, causing rotation. Reach out with your second hand and bring it down 12 inches from your first one. Just before your second hand touches the mat, extend the bent drive leg to drive your body and add to its rotation. Show flexibility in the split leg position. Land on your first leg 12 inches from your second hand while your drive leg lands 12 inches from your second hand. Continue moving forward as you go into the one-arm cartwheel. Place your second arm down 20 inches from the drive foot. Throw the thrust leg up and over as you extend the drive leg and push off the mat. Allow your legs to rotate over your head and land in a side position. Push off the mat with your arms and shoulders as your legs start down for the mat. Do a quarter turn as you go into the round-off by bending forward at the waist and at one knee, placing your hands 14 inches from your first foot. Bring your first hand in front of your body and your second hand around and behind the first. Thrust your legs up to the vertical position. As your legs reach the vertical, let your body make a half turn. Snap your legs down forcefully as your arms push and your shoulders extend, lifting your upper body as your legs go on the mat. Stand and face the direction from which you came. Sit back and bend your hips, lowering your body as you go into the back roll. From a squatting position with your chin tucked on your chest, place your head forward and round your back to form a rocker. Push off the mat and roll back. Place your hands beside your head to help take the pressure off your neck as your body weight rolls over your head. As your hands make contact with the mat behind your head, push and keep your knees tucked in tight to your chest so that you land on your feet out of the back roll.

Common Errors:

(1) Not taking a side position as you begin the cartwheel. (2) Having inadequate marking of the one, two count hand placement. (3) Placing your hands down on the one-arm cartwheel too close to the drive leg. (4) Not throwing the thrust leg and extending the drive leg together. (5) Failing to place your hands in front of your body at the beginning of the round-off. (6) Never reaching the handstand position with your legs before executing the half turn. (7) Not keeping your neck and back rounded as you go into the back roll. (8) Having improper placement of your hands by your head as your body weight passes over the base.

Coaching Points:

(1) Do the cartwheel from the side position. (2) Reach for your arm and feet placement in the cartwheel. (3) Be sure your hand is placed 20 inches from the drive foot. (4) Be sure the throw of the thrust leg and the extension of the drive leg are done together. (5) Place your first hand down directly in front of your body. (6) Put your second hand behind and to the side of your first. (7) Be sure the direction of the round-off passes through the vertical over the top. (8) Have proper placement of your hands beside your head in the back roll. (9) Round your back and tuck your chin as you go into the roll.

Practice Hints:

(1) From a standing position practice the mechanics of the thrust and drive of your legs. (2) Use a line on the mat to check the proper

hand placement and the direction of the cartwheel. (3) Use the same hints for the one-arm cartwheel as you would for a regular cartwheel. (4) Do several round-offs from a standing position before trying to put them into the series. (5) Do the skill slowly at first. (6) Review the back roll. (7) Take the first two by themselves and then the last two before putting them together.

Spotting Tips:

As you begin the cartwheel, the spotter places one hand in your mid-section as your first hand goes down. His other hand grasps your waist as your legs start going over. He can use the same spotting methods for the one-arm cartwheel as he would for the two-arm. He moves with each skill. As you go into the round-off, he checks your direction. If it is poor, he grasps your hips and pulls them in line. As you sit back going into the back roll, he lifts your hips as your body weight passes over your head.

53. One-Arm Front Walkover

Stand facing the mat. Lift the drive leg up and raise your arms to the vertical. Bend forward and place one hand down in front of your shoulders and thrust the same side throw leg up and over as you extend the drive leg pushing off the mat. Keep your arms straight and your head back as your legs pass over your hand and come down in a step-out position.

Common Errors:

(1) Placing your hand too close to your foot. (2) Having poor direction of your legs as they pass over your hands. (3) Having insufficient mechanics of the thrust and drive legs. (4) Putting your head down on the first part of the one-arm walkover.

Coaching Points:

(1) Keep your arms locked at the elbow. (2) Place your hand in front of your body and not to the side. (3) Extend the thrust and drive movements together. (4) Keep moving your body forward as you come out of the walkover.

Practice Hints:

(1) Do the skill on a stack of mats, placing your hand down on the stack and landing on the lower mat. (2) Use the spotter to assist you at your back and in coming up. (3) Place one hand on top of the other in practice for the one-arm walkover.

Spotting Tips:

As you begin the one-arm walkover and place your hand down, the spotter places one hand in the small of your back. His second one touches your throw leg. He assists in pushing your throw leg over the top, speeding up rotation. He moves with the skill to its completion.

FREE TUMBLING

Free tumbling involves the skills of basic tumbling and acrobatics. However, there is additionally a period of free flight when neither the hands nor the feet touch the mat.

54. Front Headspring

Begin from a standing position facing the mat. Bend forward at your hips and knees. Place your hands beside your head as though you were going into a headstand. As your toes leave the mat and your hips move forward, extend your legs up and over into a back bend with your feet landing 24 inches from your head. As your hips go over, push with your arms to cause a period of free flight. Let your arms follow the movement of the upper body before extending your elbows and coming to a standing position.

Common Errors:

(1) Failing to allow your hips to move forward in front of the base before extending your legs up and over into the back bend. (2) Not stretching your arms as your hips extend up and over in the period of free flight. (3) Having improper direction of your arms as the top of your body lifts to the upright position.

Coaching Points:

(1) Be sure your hips move beyond the vertical position before attempting to extend your hips over into the back bend. (2) Make sure that the extension of your arms and hips is simultaneous. (3) Have the abdominal region travel up as your feet go down to create as much bend as possible. (4) Be sure your head is back as your arms push off the mat.

Practice Hints:

(1) From a stack of mats, do a half roll with a headspring, placing your head and hands on the stacked mats while extending your hips and landing on the lower mat. (2) From a piked headstand, let your hips move beyond the base. Extend your legs up and over while pushing with your arms to land in a back bridge. From the back bridge stand up. (3) Work on a trampoline turning a half roll into a headspring.

Spotting Tips:

As you move forward and place your hands and head on the mat, the spotter places one hand in the small of your back. As you extend your legs up, over, and down his other hand grasps your shoulders following the motion of your body up into the stand. His first hand then lifts your hips and lowers your back as his second hand lifts your shoulders and head.

Front Headspring

55. Front Handspring

Stand and face the mat. Raise your arms above your head in a vertical position. Raise either leg. Simultaneously, step forward on your raised leg, bend forward at your waist, and place your hands on the mat slightly in front of your shoulders. As your hands make contact with the mat, thrust the throw leg up and over as you extend the drive leg. Place your legs together as your body passes through the vertical in the handstand. Keep your legs together as they come down on the mat simultaneously. At the same time, push off with your arms and shoulders. Stand with your arms extended and your elbows close to your ears.

Common Errors:

(1) Placing your hands too close to your feet on the take-off. (2) Not allowing your body to pass through the handstand before bending back going down. (3) Not thrusting from the arms and shoulders as the legs come down for the landing. (4) Not having proper arm patterns as you come to a standing position.

Coaching Points:

(1) Keep your arms straight and your head up as they make contact with the mat at the first of the skill. (2) Be sure that the thrust of the throw leg and the extension of the drive leg take place as soon as the hands touch the mat. (3) Be sure your feet come together as your body passes through the handstand going down. (4) Keep your arms extended and your elbows close to your ears as the top of your trunk comes up to a standing position.

Practice Hints:

(1) Take one step toward a stack of mats. (2) Place your hands on the stacked mats, and do a handspring landing on the lower mat. (3) Stand, bend forward, kick up to a handstand, and bridge into a back bend. (4) Speed up the handstand and back bend until there is a period of free flight. (5) Keep your hips up, and do not break to a sitting position. (6) Have a spotter tap your hips as they come over to help you extend them into an upright position.

Spotting Tips:

As you move forward to place your hands on the mat, the spotter places his first hand in the small of your back. As you extend your drive leg and throw your thrust leg up and over, his second hand assists you on the upper shoulders and arms to lift your body up. He follows your motion until you stand up.

Front Handspring

56. Front Handspring Stepout

From a standing position facing the mat with your arms raised vertically above your head, raise one leg. Step forward rapidly, bend from your waist and place both hands on the mat keeping your arms straight and your head up. As your hands touch the mat, thrust the throw leg up and over while you extend the drive leg up and over. As your legs reach the vertical position in the handstand, allow the thrust leg to continue forward, splitting off to let the drive leg remain behind. Arch your back and push with your arms coming into a back bend with one leg ahead of the other in a stepout fashion.

Common Errors:

(1) Placing your hands too close to your feet on the take-off. (2) Failing to extend the drive leg and throw the thrust leg simultaneously. (3) Having inadequate split of your legs as your body reaches the vertical position. (4) Having improper direction of your arms in the last phase of the handspring stepout.

Coaching Points:

(1) Place your hands in front of your shoulders going into the first phase of the handspring stepout. (2) Be sure that the thrust of the throw leg and the extension of the drive leg take place as soon as your hands touch the mat. (3) Split your legs as your body passes the vertical position with the thrust leg going forward and the drive leg remaining slightly behind. (4) Land in a stepout position with the drive leg landing last and reaching forward to move your body weight in that direction.

Practice Hints:

(1) From a stack of mats, bend forward placing your hands down to do a handstand walkout. (2) Land on the lower level. (3) Practice doing a series of front walkovers before you do the handspring stepout. (4) Have a spotter touch your hips and lift your body to obtain the feeling of free flight in the stepout. (5) Learn to do a series of front walkovers rapidly to help obtain free flight in the handspring stepout.

Spotting Tips:

As you move forward placing your hands on the mat, the spotter places one hand on the small of your back. As you extend the drive leg and throw the thrust leg up and over, his second hand assists you at your shoulders and upper arms. His first hand lifts your hips and the small of your back while his second one lifts your shoulders and upper trunk. He follows the motion until you land in a stepout.

Front Handspring Stepout

57. Kangaroo Front Walkover

Start from a standing position facing the mat. Raise your arms above your head to the vertical position. Raise one leg. Step forward vigorously, placing your hands in front of your shoulders. As you throw the thrust leg up and over and extend the drive leg, quickly move (hop) both hands forward ten inches in a one, two fashion. Allow your leg to continue up and over, coming out in a stepout.

Common Errors:

(1) Placing your hands too close to your feet when you begin the skill. (2) Hopping hands too far out as your feet pass over your head. (3) Failing to hop hands as your throw leg goes up and your drive leg extends. (4) Having inadequate direction of your arms in the last phase of the skill.

Coaching Points:

(1) Be sure your hands are placed slightly in front of your shoulders on the first touch. (2) Be sure that the distance on the hand hop is short and done as you thrust the throw leg up and extend the drive leg while your hips move up, but yet short of the vertical position. (3) As your trunk comes up, keep your head back, arms extended, elbows in close to your ears.

Practice Hints:

(1) From a front walkover, do the one, two hand hop slowly as the spotter lifts your hips. (2) Practice hopping hands before throwing the thrust leg up and extending the drive leg. (3) Mark lines on mat to determine the distance that your hands travel on the hop.

Spotting Tips:

As you come forward placing your first hand on the mat, the spotter places his first hand in the small of your back. As your arms move forward, the thrust leg goes up, and the drive extends, he places his second hand on your shoulders and upper arm region. He lifts your hips up as you make the change in your hand position to give you a period of free flight. He follows the skill with his first hand on the small of your back and his second one on your shoulders.

58. Front Mounter

From a standing position facing the mat, take several running steps. Lift the drive leg forward and bend at the knee. Swing your arms forward and up as your drive leg extends and your thrust leg goes over, causing a period of free flight on the first phase of the skill. Bring your hands down 36 inches from the drive leg and slightly in front of your shoulders. As your hands make contact with the mat, let your legs continue forward in the split position. Land with your hips extended up in a walkout fashion.

Common Errors:

(1) Failing to swing your arms up in a forward circle before placing them on the mat. (2) Failing to throw the thrust leg and extend the drive leg as your arms circle up. (3) Placing your hands too close to the take-off foot in the last part of the skill. (4) Staggering your hands as they land on the mat.

Coaching Points:

(1) Be sure that all three forces are executed simultaneously—the swinging of the arms up, the extension of the drive leg, and the throw of the thrust leg. (2) When your hands make contact with the mat, bring them in front of your shoulders. (3) Be sure that your arms are extended and locked when your hands touch the mat. (4) Keep your arms extended behind your head as they leave the mat and follow the upper body motion.

Practice Hints:

(1) From a standing position, thrust your arms forward and up, driving into a walkover. (2) Add one running step. (3) After you have the timing, add several running steps and attempt to do the entire movement, getting as much free flight as possible.

Spotting Tips:

As you travel forward swinging your arms forward and up, the spotter puts his first hand on your stomach, lifting your body up during free flight. As you bring the thrust leg over and extend the drive leg, he puts his second hand in the small of your back, aiding you in direction and in lifting your body as your hands touch the mat and body mass passes over the base. He follows the movement until you stand up.

59. Combination Front Tinsica, One-Arm Cartwheel, Back Walkover

From a standing position facing the mat, bend forward placing your first hand in front of the drive leg. As your hands touch the mat, throw the thrust leg forward and up, and extend the drive leg. As the legs are en route, reach forward with your second hand and place it in front of your first hand on the mat. Do the one, two count with your hands and keep them in a straight line. Coming out of the tinsica, execute a one-quarter turn. Keep your body weight moving forward when going into the one-arm cartwheel by placing your second hand in front of the drive leg. As your hands touch the mat, throw the thrust leg forward and up and extend the drive leg. Show as much flexibility as possible as your body passes through the vertical position, marking three counts in the one-arm cartwheel. Upon landing, do a one-quarter turn, letting your body weight shift back with your hips coming over the base using the puppet string action, raising your legs and arms while putting your head back as you go into the back bend. Be sure to extend your arms and place both hands on the mat as your first leg extends up and over in the back bend. Press with your finger tips and raise your head as the backward momentum continues. Split your legs when coming into the back walkover. Land on your first leg and extend your second one back to maintain a proper body line as you come to the standing position.

Common Errors:

(1) Failing to show a one, two count in the placement of your hands on the front tinsica. (2) Having improper direction when your hands are placed on the mat. (3) Doing a back bend rather than a quarter side bend when coming out of the tinsica. (4) Placing your second hand down too close to the drive leg in the one-arm cartwheel. (5) Having inadequate split of your legs as your hips pass through the vertical position. (6) Failing to show the three counts in the one-arm cartwheel. (7) Not having puppet string action in the lifting of your leg, arms, and head going into the back bend. (8) Failing to use your hands and head to help maintain momentum as your feet pass over the base. (9) Having improper body line coming out of the back walkover.

Coaching Points:

(1) Draw a line down the mat to show proper direction and hand placement on the front tinsica and one-arm cartwheel. (2) Mark two counts in the tinsica, three counts in the one-arm cartwheel, and three counts in the back walkover. (3) Show maximum flexibility in the leg split as your hips pass through the vertical position. (4) Try to maintain an even rhythm as you connect the front tinsica to the one-arm cartwheel to the back walkover.

Practice Hints:

(1) Work each skill separately before attempting to do the combination. (2) Review the mechanics of the three skills before doing the series. (3) Take the front tinsica and the one-arm cartwheel separately, then the one-arm cartwheel and the back walkover before putting all three together. (4) Count the mechanics of the hand placement as you do each skill.

Spotting Tips:

As you come forward, bend at your waist, and place your first hand down on the tinsica. The spotter puts his first hand on the small of your back. As your second hand goes down and your legs go up, he assists you at the shoulders with his second hand. He lifts up with his first hand on your hips and assists your shoulders with his second. As you move forward to the cartwheel, he places his first hand in your mid-section as you put your first hand down in the cartwheel. His second hand goes around your waist as your legs pass through the vertical position, aiding you by lifting your hips and giving direction to the movement. When you are going into the back walkover, the spotter places one hand in the small of your back, lowering your body into the back bend for your hand placement. He helps your first leg over into the back walkover by touching and pushing back.

AERIALS

There are three mechanics involved in aerials: (1) the thrust of the throw leg up and over, (2) the extension of the drive leg as it pushes off the mat which is done with number one, (3) the lifting up of the arms as numbers one and two are executed.

60. Aerial Cartwheel

Face the mat and take several running steps, lifting the drive leg up as you bend forward at your trunk. Violently thrust the throw leg up and over. At the same time push off the mat with the drive leg to establish rotation. Look up to establish a high moment of rotation as your hips pass beyond the vertical going over. Follow through with your arms swinging down and up to make all three forces prevalent.

Common Errors:

(1) Not extending the drive leg as the thrust leg is thrown up and over. (2) Bending your body forward as you place the drive leg on the mat too far forward. (3) Having inadequate extension of the drive leg.

Coaching Points:

(1) As the drive leg goes on the mat, try to hold the upper portion of your body in an erect position. (2) Be sure the thrust leg remains extended throughout its entire flight in the cartwheel. (3) Focus on an object as you move into the aerial cartwheel to keep the top part of your body from being too slow.

Practice Hints:

(1) Off a stack of mats practice the one-arm cartwheel with your second arm landing on the lower mat. (2) In executing a one-arm cartwheel off the stack of mats, think of the mechanics involved in the throw of the thrust leg and the extension of the drive leg. (3) Do the cartwheel by just touching the mat with your finger tips and lifting your hand off the mat as soon as possible. (4) Have a spotter spot you carefully when doing your first aerial cartwheel.

Spotting Tips:

As you move forward and raise the drive leg, the spotter places his first hand on your mid-section. As you throw the thrust leg up and

Aerial Cartwheel

over and extend the drive leg, he lifts your mid-section, giving your hips lift while his second hand taps the throw leg as it comes up and over. He follows the movements until you stand erect.

61. Aerial Walkover

Begin from a standing position facing the mat. Take several running steps, bending slightly forward at the waist as you lift the drive leg up. Extend the thrust leg up and over. At the same time push the drive leg off the mat, lifting your arms back and up and rotating them in the air. Land in a walkout position with the thrust leg coming down first and the drive leg following. Keep your head up throughout this skill.

Common Errors:

(1) Bending forward at your waist before extending the drive leg to thrust the throw leg. (2) Failing to exert the first two forces simultaneously—the thrust of the throw leg and the extension of the drive leg. (3) Ducking your head as the thrust leg and drive leg extend. (4) Lacking flexibility in your back as your legs come down for a one, two landing.

Coaching Points:

(1) Keep your head up as the thrust leg extends up and over and the drive leg pushes off the mat. (2) Swing your arms back and up as the first two forces establish rotation. (3) Use flexibility in the back to help the rotation and landing position of your feet. (4) Remember that the mechanics of an aerial walkover are similar to the aerial cartwheel except for direction, take-off, and landing.

Practice Hints:

(1) Use a stack of mats. Begin by thrusting the throw leg and extending the drive leg off a stack of mats, landing on the lower level after the period of free flight to aid in rotation as your body comes in line for the landing. (2) Do several handspring stepouts rapidly. (3) Keep your head up and spot some object in order to assure the proper head position as your legs rotate over your body in the aerial walkover. (4) Use a spotter to tap the throw leg as it turns over, and to lend support at the small of your back.

Spotting Tips:

The spotter stands to the side in front of you. As you extend the thrust leg and push the drive leg, he puts his first hand on the small of your back. His second hand taps the throw leg as it passes over the top. He follows the movement with his first hand on the small of your back until you have landed on your feet.

Aerial Walkover

62. Back Handspring

Begin with your back to the mat, facing outward. Think of sitting in a chair with bent knees and sitting back on your hips while keeping the upper part of your body at a right angle with your hips. As your body begins to lose balance and fall back, swing your arms up, drop your head back, and extend your hips up. Push with your legs as hands touch the mat. Keep your hips extended until your body has reached the vertical position. Then break from your waist while sharply snapping your legs down and pushing with your arms as you raise your head. Bring the upper portion of your body up as your legs come down for the landing. Do two counts for the back handspring. Bring your hands down first, then your feet.

Common Errors:

(1) Failing to sit back with your body weight before extending your hips up when going into the back handspring. (2) Extending your hips forward rather than back and up. (3) Having inadequate thrust up and over with your arms as you begin the back handspring. (4) Breaking your hips on the snapdown before your body reaches the vertical position.

Coaching Points:

(1) Sit back as you extend your hips when going into the back handspring. (2) Have your eyes follow your arms and hands as they go up, back, and over. (3) Keep your hips in an extended position until your body is in the vertical before breaking for the snapdown. (4) As your hips break from the vertical position, push off with your arms and shoulders, lifting the top part of your body.

Practice Hints:

(1) Facing a wall, sit back as if you were going into a handspring. (2) Work from a stack of mats as you sit back, executing the thrust of your arms and head back and up while extending your hips and placing your hands on the lower mat. (3) Allow the period between the two heights to give your body a chance to move into the proper position for the handspring. (4) Use spotting assistance on the small of your back and your legs to learn the proper mechanics and the one, two count for the hands and feet—first hands, then feet.

Spotting Tips:

As you sit back, the spotter places one hand under your hips and the other on the small of your back. As you swing your arms up, drop your head back and extend your hips for the back bend. He follows the movement, keeping his arms in the same portion of your body. He helps you extend your hips by pushing your legs up and by pushing on the small of your back as you go into the inverted postion toward the vertical. As your hips reach the vertical position and you bend at the waist, he releases your body as you snap down for the landing.

78

63. Combination Round-off, Back Handspring

Facing the mat take several running steps, bending forward at your waist as you place your hands down simultaneously, your first hand reaching in front of your drive leg and your second reaching around behind your first one. Touch the mats simultaneously with your hands as you throw the thrust leg up and over while you extend the drive leg. As your body reaches the vertical position, execute a half turn with your hips ending in the direction from which you came. From the vertical position, snap your hips down. Shrug and push with your arms and shoulders to lift the top portion of your body to an upright position. From this position, shift your body weight back as the top portion of your body leans back, bringing your hips to a sitting position as if you were in a chair. Swing your arms up and over as your head follows. Extend your hips up and back with your legs driving off the mat and your hands landing on the mat as your body comes to the vertical position in the back handspring. From the vertical position your hips break coming down, and your arms and shoulders push from the mat, causing the upper portion of your body to rise as your legs drive toward the mats to execute a round-off back handspring.

Common Errors:

(1) Placing your hands improperly when going into the round-off. (2) Having inadequate thrust of your arms and shoulders as your legs snap down when coming out of the round-off. (3) Failing to lift the top portion of your body as your legs drive toward the mat, which causes an inadequate position going into the handspring. (4) Breaking your hips, causing the legs to be driven down before your body reaches the vertical position, which causes a shortening of the radius as your legs pass through the vertical position.

Coaching Points:

(1) Place your hands directly in front of the drive leg when going into the round-off. (2) Be sure your center of gravity is well behind the base before extending your hips up and back when going into the back handspring. (3) Mark a one, two count on the round-off and a three, four count on the back handspring. (4) Be sure your body reaches the extended position in the vertical before your hips break coming out of the round-off back handspring. This causes proper rotation of the upper part of your body when coming to the upright position.

Practice Hints:

(1) Draw a line down the mat. Begin with a round-off back handspring and try to keep the direction of the skills going straight down the line. (2) Practice the skills separately before putting them in a

combination. (3) Use the assistance of a spotter when first attempting these skills. (4) From a standing position, kick up into a handstand. As your body reaches a vertical position, break from your hips, snapping your legs down and pushing with your shoulders. Go into a back handspring, breaking down the mechanics of a round-off back handspring.

Spotting Tips:

The spotter stands in front of you to your side. As you break for the mat he moves close, following your body through the mechanics of a round-off by placing his first hand on the small of your back and his second hand behind your thighs. As you bend back and extend your hips up and over, he puts his first hand on the small of your back and his second hand on your thigh, giving you support as you extend your hips up and over. He taps your legs causing the rotation to be completed as you pass beyond the vertical position, snapping the round-off back handspring. His hands follow your motion until you have come to a standing position.

64. Combination Front Handspring Stepout, Front Handspring

From a standing position facing the mat, take several running steps. Bend forward from your waist, lifting the drive leg up. Place your hands on the mat slightly in front of your shoulders. As your hands touch the mat, extend the throw leg up and over while you push the drive leg and lift the body up. As your legs pass the vertical position, let the throw leg continue ahead while the drive leg stays behind. Push with your arms from the shoulders. Drop your head behind. Extend your arms and keep your elbows close to your ears as your body lands with a period of free flight from the time your hands leave the mat until the landing of your first leg. Continue your body momentum forward, placing your hands slightly in front of your shoulders while keeping your head up and locking your arms. Extend the throw leg up and over as you push the drive leg off the pad. Put your feet together in the vertical position. Arch your back as your feet land on the mat simultaneously. Push with the arms, keep your head back, and keep your elbows close to the ears. You will also have a period of free flight in the second phase from the time the hands leave the mat until the feet land on the pad for the front handspring.

Common Errors:

(1) Placing your hands too close to your feet on the take-off of the front stepout. (2) Failing to coordinate the extension of the drive leg and the thrust of the throw leg to a simultaneous explosion when going into the front handspring stepout. (3) Failing to keep your body

moving forward after the conclusion of the front handspring stepout. (4) Having an improper arm pattern coming out of the front handspring stepout and the front handspring. (5) Failing to extend your arms and keep your elbows close to your ears and behind your head.

Coaching Points:

(1) Place your hands slightly in front of your shoulders while going into the front handspring stepout and the front handspring. (2) At the conclusion of the front handspring stepout, be sure to keep your body movement going forward as you bend from your waist when placing your hands down going into the front handspring. (3) Be sure that the extension of the drive leg and the thrust of the throw leg are executed simultaneously to get the maximum use out of both forces. (4) Keep your arms extended and your elbows close to your ears when coming up to the standing position. (5) Show as much free flight from the time your hands touch the pad until your feet land in the front handspring stepout as in the front handspring.

Practice Hints:

(1) Do both skills, the front handspring stepout and the front handspring, separately before trying to put them in a combination. (2) Work both skills separately from a stack of mats. (3) Land with your legs on the lower pad. (4) Enlist a spotter to place his hands on the small of your back and on your shoulders when coming out of the handspring stepout.

Spotting Tips:

The spotter stands to the side in front of you. As you run for the mat, bending forward at the waist and placing your first hand down, he places his first hand on the small of your back. His second hand supports your shoulders. He follows the movement of your body to the upright position. His first hand lifts your hips while his second hand keeps your shoulders erect as you come into a standing position. As you go into the front handspring, he takes the same position as he did in the first phase, with his first hand going on the small of your back and his second hand beneath your shoulders. He then lifts your hips and puts your shoulders in the right projection as you come up to a standing position.

65. Combination Cartwheel, Aerial Cartwheel

Face outward from a standing sideways position on the mat. Raise the drive leg up and place your first hand down in a low oblique position while your second hand goes to the vertical position beside your head. Bend sideways from your waist, placing your first hand 14 inches from your feet while thrusting the throw leg up and over as you complete the rotation of the drive leg. Reach out with your second hand 14 inches from your first hand. Show as much flexibility as possible as your legs pass through the vertical position. Finish the first phase of the cartwheel with four counts. Keep your body weight and momentum moving forward as you go into the aerial cartwheel. As your head and shoulders move forward beyond the base, throw the thrust leg violently as you extend the drive leg. Lift your arms back and up as your body rotates in the air, executing the aerial cartwheel coming out in a side landing position.

Common Errors:

(1) Placing your hands too close to your feet on the take-off of the cartwheel. (2) Failing to mark four distinct counts on the cartwheel with your hands and feet. (3) Attempting to do the aerial cartwheel before your body weight passes beyond the base when going into the skill. (4) Having inadequate thrust of the throw leg and extension of the drive leg as you push off the mat. (5) Bending the upper part of your body too low when going into the aerial.

Coaching Points:

(1) Mark four distinct counts in the cartwheel. (2) Be sure that your body weight is in proper position before trying to do the aerial cartwheel. (3) Remember the importance of combining the extension of the drive leg and the thrust of the throw leg when going into the aerial. (4) Remember that your body lands in a side position at the end of the series.

Practice Hints:

(1) Do the cartwheel and the aerial cartwheel separately before attempting to put them together. (2) Review the mechanics of the cartwheel before doing the aerial. (3) Work the aerial cartwheel several time off a stack of mats and land on the lower mat using the extra height as a period of flight to allow your body to come into the proper perspective for landing. (4) Use a spotter when transferring your body weight from the cartwheel to the aerial cartwheel. Have him assist you in the aerial by lifting the upper part of your body with his first hand and tapping the throw leg with his second.

Spotting Tips:

The spotter stands to the side in front of you. As you go into the cartwheel, he places his first hand in your mid-section. He lifts up to give elevation to the top of your body. As your thrust leg extends up and over, he taps your first leg, establishing rotation. He follows your movement ready to assist you when going into the aerial, and places his first hand on your mid-section, lifting up on your body to give it elevation at the top. He taps your throw leg as it comes up and over, and follows the movement of the aerial until you have landed.

66. Combination Front Handspring Stepout, Round-off Back Handspring

From a standing position facing the mat, take several running steps. Lift the drive leg up as you swing your arms up to the vertical position. Bend forward at your waist, placing your hands down slightly in front of your shoulders. As your hands touch the mat, extend the drive leg off of it as you throw the thrust leg back and up to establish rotation. Let your body continue forward and over with your legs split. As your hips pass the vertical position, shove with your arms and shoulders causing a momentary period of free flight before your feet land on the mat. With your body weight moving forward, continue to a stepout position and place your hand in front of the drive foot for the round-off. Put your hands down simultaneously with your first hand in front of the drive foot and your second hand around and behind your other hand. Bring your throw leg up as the drive leg extends from the pad. Put your feet together in a vertical position, executing a half twist. Snap your legs down, landing in the same direction from which you came. As your legs break coming down, push from your arms and shrug your shoulders to raise the top part of your body, thus completing the round-off. Upon the conclusion of the round-off, shift your weight back by letting your hips go back and form a right angle with the upper portion of your body. Swing your arms up and back. As you lose your balance, extend your hips up and back, placing your hands on the mat with your body in a back bend. Push off the mat with your legs as your feet come to the vertical position. Break from your hips, snapping downward. Push from your shoulders to come to an erect standing position.

Common Errors:

(1) Placing your hands too close to your feet on the front handspring stepout. (2) Failing to keep your body weight moving forward after the front handspring stepout when going into the round-off. (3) Doing a one-half twist too soon at the top of the round-off. (4) Failing to let your hips pass beyond the base before thrusting them up and back when going into the front handspring. (5) Failing to mark the two counts of the front handspring step-out, the two counts for your hands and feet when landing in the round-off, and the two counts for your feet when landing in the back handspring.

Coaching Points:

(1) Remember to place your hands on the mats slightly in front of your shoulders when going into the front handspring stepout. (2) Extend the drive leg and throw the thrust leg up and over as your hands make contact with the mat, causing elevation and rotation in the front handspring stepout. (3) Keep your body weight moving forward as you come out of the handspring stepout when going into

the round-off. (4) Be sure that you do the half turn while your body is in the vertical position. (5) Be sure that your body weight is beyond the base and the upper portion of your body is extended to a right angle with your thighs before you extend your hips up and back. Swing your head and arms up when you go into the back handspring.

Practice Hints:

(1) Execute each of the skills individually before trying to combine them. (2) Work the front handspring stepout into the round-off. Then work the round-off and back handspring before putting them into a combination. (3) Use a spotter to assure the proper technique and your safety.

Spotting Tips:

The spotter stands to the side in front of you. As you break for the mat, he places his first hand on the small of your back as you place your hands on the mat and lift your hips over. His second hand goes by your shoulders, giving aid to the upper portion of your body as you come out of the handspring front stepout to an upright position. As you go into the round-off he places his hand in your mid-section when you reach the vertical position while executing the half turn snap-down. He moves back as you sit back going into the back handspring. He places his first hand on the small of your back and his second hand below your thighs. As you sit back going into the back handspring, he lifts and elevates the upper portion of your body with one hand while his other one aids your legs as you lift them up to the vertical position before snapping them down.

67. Combination Back Handspring, Back Handspring

Begin with your back to the mat facing outward. Establish a sitting position by bending back and lowering the upper portion of your body to form a right angle with your hips while your body weight goes beyond the base. As you come to the off-balance position, thrust your arms up, back, and over as your head follows and you extend your hips to do a back bend. As your hands make contact with the mat, push off with your legs to reach a vertical position. From this position break your hips sharply as your legs continue down. Push with your arms and shoulders, causing the upper portion of your body to come to an upright position. Do the second handspring the same way as you did the first one.

Common Errors:

(1) Failing to hold your body weight back beyond the base before you attempt to extend your hips and swing your arms up and over in the first phase of the back handspring. (2) Bending your hips allowing

your legs to start down before they have reached the vertical position in the back handspring. (3) Having inadequate thrust from your arms and shoulders as your legs come down and your upper body rises to a standing position. (4) Failing to allow your body weight to pass beyond the base before going into the second handspring.

Coaching Points:

(1) Review the mechanics of a back handspring before doing the skill. (2) Use the aid of a spotter when going from one handspring into the other. (3) When you begin the handspring series, work from a stack of mats doing the back handspring off them. Place your hands on the lower level to allow a period of free flight between the heights of the mats in order to establish enough momentum to go from one handspring into the other.

Spotting Tips:

As your body weight shifts back beyond the base, the spotter aids you with his first hand on the small of your back while he places his second hand behind your thighs. As you swing your arms up and back, and you extend your hips up and over, he lifts the top of your body with his first hand and pushes your leg up and over with his second one helping to establish rotation and extension of your hips. He follows your motion throughout the skill aiding you to come to a standing position.

68. Standing Back Somersault in Tucked Position

From a standing position with back to mat, bend your knees slightly and bring your arms down and swing them up. Put your head back as you extend your legs when coming off the mat to lift your body up to a vertical position. Continue moving your arms and head back and over. As you lift your body up in a back dive position, bend your knees up toward your chest, making sure that your knees come up to join your arms rather than that your arms and head bend forward and down to your knees. Do a back tucked somersault by keeping your head back and bringing your knees over the top, rotating as your body passes beyond the vertical position and starts down. Keep your head circling up. As your legs pass directly below it, extend from the tucked position and drive your legs down onto the mat.

Common Errors:

(1) Failing to lift your arms above your head to lift your body up in the first phase of the flight. (2) Bending your head forward, ducking it, and bringing it in the direction of the knees rather than your knees following your head. (3) Having too loose a tuck as your body rotates

Standing Back Somersault in Tucked Position

back. (4) Failing to keep your knees and ankles in contact wi
body until your legs are under you.

Coaching Points:

(1) Be sure that the mechanics of your head and arms are up and
back. (2) Continue this motion throughout the back tucked somersault. (3) Push off the mat with your legs, attempting to get maximum
altitude before executing the back somersault. (4) Remain in a tight
tucked position until your body has rotated beyond the vertical and
your legs are directly under it for the landing.

Practice Hints:

(1) Do the back tucked somersault from a stack of mats, landing
on the lower level. (2) Use a spotter to lift your hips up to rotate them
in the beginning. (3) Remember that the mechanics are up, not back,
so that the elevation is up and down. (4) In the beginning practice
a standing back somersault on a trampoline or off a minitramp.

Spotting Tips:

As you swing your arms and head up, extend your legs, and lift
your body up to the vertical position, the spotter places one hand on
the small of your back and his other beneath your hips on the back
side of your thighs. His first hand gives elevation to the top of your
body and supports the small of your back as you tuck knees in rotating
over the top. His second hand lifts your knees toward your chest
causing you to turn over into a back somersault. He follows your
movement until you have landed safely.

69. Front Somersault Tucked Position

Begin from a standing position facing the mat. Bring your arms
forward and up as your legs extend from the mat, causing your body
to rise up and forward. Just before your body reaches the top of the
piked flight, tuck your chin on your chest, swing your arms forward
and down and cut your legs from under you by tucking your knees
in tight to your chest. Establish rotation by ducking your head and
swinging your arms forward and down. Rotate forward in a somersault position, freely suspended, coming out of the somersault as your
legs pass directly below your head. Extend your body from the tucked
position with your legs reaching down to land on the mat.

Common Errors:

(1) Diving too far forward and out. (2) Having an inadequate tuck
as your body rotates forward and over in the somersault. (3) Failing
to coordinate the swinging of your arms, the ducking of your head,
and the tucking of your legs to establish proper rotation for the somersault. (4) Having inadequate extension of your legs as your body rotation enables you to come to a standing position.

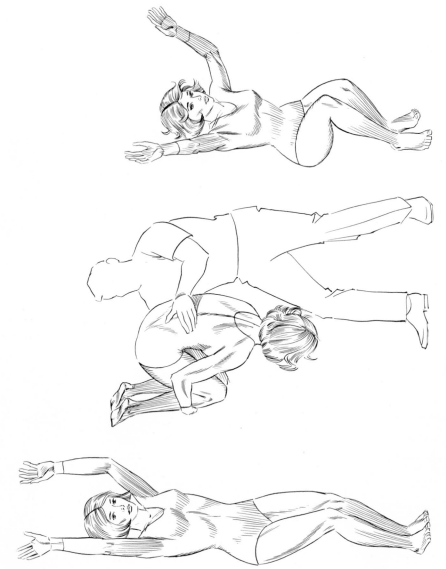

Front Somersault Tucked Position

Coaching Points:

(1) Dive up rather than out for elevation and height. (2) Swing your arms down, tuck chin, tuck knees tightly to your body to establish rotation. (3) Extend your legs vigorously as the rotation nears completion and point your feet toward the mat.

Practice Hints:

(1) From a standing position on a stack of mats execute the front somersault, rotating forward, over, and down to land on the lower level. (2) Use the mechanics of a tight tuck forward roll. (3) Do a front somersault in a tucked position into a well padded landing area. (4) Use a spotter in rotating to help you land in the proper position.

Spotting Tips:

The spotter stands to the side in front of you. As you swing your arms up, he places his first hand on your mid-section. As you swing your arms forward and down after you have extended your legs lifting your body up, he places his second hand on the small of your back to aid in rotation and to lift your hips. As you rotate, he grasps your waist holding your body up tightly to allow your legs to rotate in the landing direction. He follows your movement until you have completed the rotation.

70. Front Somersault Stepout Position

Begin from a standing position facing the mat. Swing your arms forward and up as you extend your legs to lift your body forward and up. Just before your body reaches maximum height, tuck your chin and swing your arms up and down. As your arms touch your knees pull them tightly to your chest, creating a tucked position of your body. After you have done three-quarters of the somersault, extend your legs in a split position, placing one down while reaching forward with your second one to create a stepout or walkout landing.

Common Errors:

(1) Diving too far out instead of up when you lift your body in the first phase. (2) Having an inadequate tuck position in the first three-quarters of the somersault. (3) Failing to extend your legs in the stepout position. (4) Splitting your legs too soon before your body is in the proper position to do the stepout.

Coaching Points:

(1) From a stack of mats, do a front somersault stepout, landing on the lower level of mats to use the free flight to improve the skill. (2) Remember the mechanics of your arms and head as your body lifts up off the mat. (3) After your hips come into position, tuck your head and swing your arms forward and down to establish rotation. (4) Remember the upward flight pattern of your body. (5) When your legs

pass the vertical position, split them by extending one forward and the other one down when coming out in a stepout.

Practice Hints:

(1) From a stack of mats, take several running steps using a double foot take-off. Push off. As your body lifts for rotation, do a front somersault stepout landing on the lower level of mats, using the difference in height to give your body time to rotate into the proper position for landing. (2) Use a spotter when doing the front somersault stepout. (3) Review the mechanics of your head and arms as your body lifts for the rotation in the front somersault.

Spotting Tips:

The spotter stands to the side in front of you. As you take several running steps and begin the double foot take-off, he places one hand on your mid-section as you swing your arms up and extend your legs to drive your body upward to the vertical. As you duck your head and swing your arms forward and down, begin rotation, and tuck your knees, he places his second hand in the small of your back to rotate and turn you over, and assists you until you land.

71. Combination Front Handspring, Front Somersault

From a standing position facing the mat, take several running steps. Swing your arms up and stretch your body, lifting the drive leg forward. Place your hands slightly in front of your shoulders as you thrust the throw leg up and over and extend the drive leg. Bring your legs together at the vertical and snap down from your hips when coming forward. As your legs pass the vertical position going down, push from your arms and shoulders keeping your head back and lifting the top part of your body up. Upon landing, be sure that your body weight moves beyond the base before going into the front somersault. Swing your arms forward and up and lift your body by extending your legs up to the vertical. As you raise your hips, tuck your head, swing your arms forward and down, and bring your knees in close to your chest, executing a front somersault in the tucked position. As your legs pass beyond the vertical going down, stretch them as they come directly beneath your body on the mat for the landing.

Common Errors:

(1) Placing your hands too close to your feet on take-off while executing the front handspring. (2) Doing your flight in the front handspring too much out, not enough up, for the driving position into the front somersault. (3) Failing to wait for your body weight to pass beyond the base after coming out of the front handspring before going

into the front somersault. (4) Having an inadequate tuck in lifting coming off the mat as you execute the front somersault.

Coaching Points:

(1) Place your hand slightly in front of your shoulders and be sure that the extension of the drive leg and the thrust of the throw leg are done together when you go into the front handspring. (2) Create a long, flat period of flight in the front handspring. (3) Bring your feet down sharply and close to the base as your body moves forward for the front somersault. (4) When driving out of the front handspring and when lifting your body up for the front somersault, make the direction to the vertical. (5) Execute a tight tuck position as your body rotates forward going into the front somersault.

Practice Hints:

(1) From a stack of mats, repeat the front handspring several times. (2) On regular mats work the front handspring with the approach causing your feet to come close to your hands. (3) Jump and assume the position for the front somersault without doing it. (4) Use the aid of a spotter while executing the front handspring and front somersault. (5) Do a standing front somersault on a trampoline or a minitramp to review the rotation and the mechanics of a front handspring, front somersault.

Spotting Tips:

The spotter stands to the side in front of you. As you break toward the mat, place your hands down, and swing your legs up and over, he places one hand on the small of your back and his other one on your shoulder. He gives elevation with his first hand and lifts your shoulders and head with his second. As you land out of the handspring and go into the front somersault, he moves forward. As you lift your body off the floor, he places his first hand on your mid-section. As your body and hips turn over the top in the tucked position, he places his second hand on the small of your back to aid you in rotation and to hold your body in position until you land.

72. Combination Back Handspring, Back Somersault in Tucked Position

Begin from a standing position with your back to the mat. Sit back by lowering your hips while keeping the top of your body upright. As you lose your balance, swing your arms forward, up and back with your head following the flight of your arms. Extend your hips up and over, pushing with your legs. As your hands touch the mat, raise your legs to the vertical position. Break at your hips and extend your legs, causing the legs to come downward. Push with the arms and shoulders, causing the upper portion of your body to rise to the vertical position. Upon landing, swing your arms up and extend your legs and head back to lift your body up. As you bring your hips into position, tuck your knees to your chest to cause your body to rotate over and back. When you bring your legs beyond the top and down and when they are in position, extend your legs from the tuck position down to the mat for landing.

Common Errors:

(1) Failing to lean your body weight back as you go into the first phase of the handspring. (2) Breaking your hips before they reach the vertical position as your legs start on down out of the handspring. (3) Failing to have the elevation for the back somersault tuck up to the vertical to give sufficient height for the skill. (4) Having an inadequate tuck in the back somersault.

Coaching Points:

(1) Sit back before executing the first phase of the handspring. (2) Be sure your hips are in the vertical position before breaking at your waist to snap the legs down in the second part of the back handspring. (3) Push with your arms as your legs snap down, causing the top part of your body to go up. (4) Swing your arms up as you put your head back and drop your legs off the mat to do a high tucked back somersault. (5) Keep a tight tucked position as your body rotates back into the somersault.

Practice Hints:

Warm up by doing a back handspring from a stack of mats to a lower level, using the difference in height to aid your body in maintaining the proper position. (2) Work with the aid of a spotter. (3) Review a standing back tucked somersault before trying to put it into a combination. (4) Do the series on the bed or a trampoline, using the free flight to give you confidence in putting the skills together.

Spotting Tips:

As you shift your body weight back when going into the back handspring, the spotter places his first hand on the small of your back. As you swing your arms up, put your head back, and extend your hips up and over, he puts his second hand behind your back on your thighs. His first hand gives lift and elevation to the top of your body while his second hand aids the rotation of your legs by tapping them as they go to the vertical position and snap down. He moves back to aid you in the back somersault. As you take off swinging your arms up, putting your head back, and extending your legs, he puts his first hand on the small of your back and his second behind you beneath your thighs. As you lift up and over, he gives elevation to the top of your body with one hand while his other aids the rotation by pushing your legs over and down. He follows you until you have landed.

73. Combination Round-off, Back Handspring, Back Somersault in Tucked Position

Begin from a standing position facing the mat. Take several running steps swinging your arms up and stretching your body out. Raise the drive leg up and forward. Bend forward at your waist, placing your hands down together with your first hand directly in front of the drive foot and your second hand over and behind the first hand. As you reach a vertical position, do a half turn snapping your legs down and pushing with your arms to lift the top of your body. Following the round-off, shift your body weight back. When your hips are in position, your body begins to lose balance. Swing your arms and head up and back. Extend your hips, pushing with your legs. Place your hands down as your legs push off the mat. Come to the vertical. Break your hips to cause their down-flight. Push with your arms and shoulders to raise up the top of your body. When you land erectly out of the back handspring, swing your arms up, put your head back, and push your legs off the mat to lift your body in the vertical direction. As your hips rise, tuck your knees to your chest rotating back from the head throw. Turn over and land on your feet.

Common Errors:

(1) Placing your hands to the side rather than straight ahead in the round-off. (2) Doing the half turn in the round-off after your legs have passed the vertical position. (3) Failing to wait until your body weight is in proper position before going into the back handspring. (4) Thrusting your hips forward rather than back and upward in the back handspring. (5) Having an inadequate snap-down when coming out of the back handspring. (6) Having the arm throw and head lift back rather than up in the first phase of the back tuck somersault. (7) Lacking a tuck position as your body rotates back into the back tuck somersault.

Coaching Points:

(1) Place your hands down in front of your first foot as you go into the round-off. (2) Do a half turn as your legs come together to approach the vertical position in the first half of the round-off. (3) Wait until your body weight has passed beyond the base and is moving back before you swing your arms, put your head back, and extend your hips up going into the back handspring. (4) On the snap-down, be sure that your legs come close to your hands. Push off with your hands lifting the upper portion of your body into the vertical position. (5) Use the proper mechanics while executing the back tuck somersault by swinging your arms straight up and lifting your head back.

Practice Hints:

(1) Do the round-off, back handspring as a separate series; then do the back handspring, back tuck somersault before putting them together. (2) Review the mechanics of each skill in the series separately. (3) Use a spotter when doing the first few passes of the round-off, back handspring, and back tuck somersault.

Spotting Tips:

The spotter stands at the side in front of you. As you run for the mat and place your hands down for the round-off position, he places his hand on your mid-section as your legs reach the vertical position, executing a half turn when coming down. He moves back for the back handspring. He places one hand on the small of your back as you set your hips back and swing your arms, put your head back and extend your hips. His other hand goes behind your thighs helping to rotate your legs over. He moves back for the back somersault, and places his first hand on the small of your back giving lift and elevation to the top portion of your body. He places his second hand behind your thighs to aid in rotation as you go up, back, and over into the somersault as he follows your movements to give you aid if necessary.

74. Combination Round-off, Back Handspring, Back Somersault in Layout Position

From a standing position facing the mat, take several running steps. Swing your arms up and bend forward at your waist. Place both hands down in front of the drive foot. Extend the thrust leg up and push your other leg off the mat. As your legs pass the vertical, do a half turn. Snap your legs down out of the round-off. Allow your body weight to move back beyond the base. Swing your arms up, pushing with your legs. As your hands touch the mat, bring your feet up to the vertical. Break your hips and snap them down. Push with your arms and shoulders, bringing the top portion of your body to the vertical position for the layout somersault. As your body weight moves out of the handspring, swing your arms up as your head goes back. Push your hips forward and up. Arch your back and push with your legs to lay your body out as it rotates freely into the layout somersault. Land on the mat with both feet.

Common Errors:

(1) Placing your hands to the side rather than straight ahead of the drive foot going into the round-off. (2) Failing to execute a half turn in the round-off as your legs pass through the vertical. (3) Failing to allow your body weight to move beyond the base out of the round-off. (4) Having inadequate snap-down of your legs and push of your

shoulders when coming out of the back handspring. (5) Carrying the back somersault layout back rather than forward and up.

Coaching Points:

(1) Place your hands in front of the drive leg. (2) Do a half turn in the round-off as your legs pass through the vertical position. (3) Allow your body weight to go beyond the base before extending your hips, throwing your arms back and your head up when going into the back handspring. (4) As your hips break out of the handspring, push from your arms and shrug your shoulders giving proper lift to your upper body. (5) Swing your arms and head up and back as your hips thrust forward and up to get the proper angle of take-off before going into the layout back somersault.

Practice Hints:

(1) Review the mechanics of each of the skills before putting them in a series. (2) Work with the aid of a spotter when doing the back handspring, back layout somersault. (3) Do a back handspring, back somersault layout on the trampoline using the bounce to execute the skill and review the mechanics before trying to do it on the mats.

Spotting Tips:

The spotter stands to the side in front of you. As you place your hands down for the round-off, he places one hand on your mid-section as your legs pass the vertical position executing the half twist, then snapping down. He moves back for the back handspring. He places his first hand on the small of your back as you swing your arms up, put your head back, and extend your hips. He puts his second hand behind your thighs to aid the rotation of your legs as they go to the vertical position and then snap down. He moves back for the back somersault layout. He places his first hand on the small of your back as you swing your arms up, put your head back, and lift your hips forward and back. His second hand moves behind your thighs, lifting your hips and rotating your body as it turns over in a layout position.

75. Combination Back Dive with a Half Twist, Forward Roll

From a standing position with your back to the mat, swing your arms up and over as you put your head back and extend your legs doing a back dive. When you suspend your body, look over either shoulder, depending on what direction you wish to twist for a half turn in the air. As your head and shoulders come down, place your hands in front of them. Duck your head slowly by allowing your body weight to roll on the back of your neck, your shoulders, and the small of your back. Finish in a standing position.

Common Errors:

(1) Beginning the twist before your feet leave the mat in the first phase of the back dive. (2) Diving back and flat rather than up. (3) Having improper position of your hips as your hands and head come down to the mat for the back roll. (4) Failing to round your back at the end of the back dive with the half twist.

Coaching Points:

(1) Do the back dive in the air before trying the half twist. (2) In the twisting process, look to the right or left and drop the same shoulder to do the half twist while your body is in the air. (3) Be sure your hips are beyond your shoulder as your body comes down going into the forward roll.

Practice Hints:

(1) Use the aid of a spotter when doing a back dive with a half twist. (2) From a stack of mats, do the back dive with a half twist to a lower level of mats for extra padding on the landing. (3) Work the mechanics of the back dive with a half twist, forward roll on a trampoline before doing the skill on the mats.

Spotting Tips:

As you swing your arms up and back, raise your head, and push off the mat with your legs to execute a back dive, the spotter places both hands out. As you do the half twist, he places his hands on your mid-section, cradling your body. As your body weight moves beyond the back dive and starts down with a half twist into the forward roll, he holds your hips and legs up with your head and shoulders in the proper position. He then allows you to come forward rolling down.

76. Round-off Back Dive with a Half Twist, Forward Roll

From a standing position facing the mat, take several running steps. Lift your arms up and bring the drive leg up. Bend forward at your waist and place your hands down in front of the drive foot. Place your first hand in front of the drive foot and your second hand around behind the first one. Thrust your legs up. As they reach the vertical position, execute a half turn. Snap your legs down and push from your arms and shoulders to bring the upper part of your body to an erect position. Upon landing out of the round-off, swing your arms and head up and back. Lift your hips forward and up. Push with your legs, executing a back dive. As you suspend, drop the shoulder on the side you twist. Look in the same direction. Do a half twist. As your body comes down from the dive and half twist, place your hands on the mat. Duck your head gradually. Allow your body to recover by rolling down the back of your neck, shoulders, the small of your back, and your legs in a forward roll.

Common Errors:

(1) Failing to place your hands in front of your first leg in the round-off. (2) Not doing a half turn as your legs reach the vertical position. (3) Failing to put your body weight in the proper position before swinging your arms up and lifting your head back for the back dive. (4) Executing the half twist before your body lifts freely from the mat in the back dive. (5) Doing the dive out rather than up.

Coaching Points:

(1) Place your first hand down in front of the drive leg and slightly in front of your shoulders. Place your second hand around behind the first one. (2) Execute the half twist of your hips as your legs pass through the vertical position. (3) While you snap your legs when coming out of the round-off, push your arms and shoulders to put the upper portion of your body in position for the back dive. (4) Swing your arms and head up as you push your hips forward and up, executing a back dive before doing the twist. (5) Be sure to look to the same side as the dropped shoulder in the half twist. (6) Remember that the direction of the back dive with the half twist is up rather than out and that your body must be in a proper angle for the forward roll.

Practice Hints:

(1) Do the round-off with a back dive half twist into a stack of mats or foam rubber. (2) Execute a back dive with a half twist from a standing position with the aid of a spotter. (3) Do a back dive with a half twist to a front drop on a trampoline before doing it on tumbling mats.

Spotting Tips:

The spotter stands to the side in front of you. As you place your hands down for the round-off, he puts one hand on your mid-section to assist your body as your hips and legs pass the vertical position executing the half turn. He moves back for the back dive. As your arms swing up and back, your head goes over, and your hips move forward and up, he cradles your body at the small of your back. As you execute a half turn, your body will turn on the front side in his arms. He holds your body in position until your head and shoulders are in proper relationship for recovering from the forward roll.

77. Combination Round-off, Back Handspring, Back Dive with Half Twist, Forward Roll

From a standing position facing the mat, take several running steps swinging your arms up to the vertical position, raising the drive leg up, bending forward at your waist, and placing both hands down. Place your first hand in front of the drive foot and your second hand around and behind the first one. Thrust your legs up. As your hips and legs reach a vertical position, do a half turn. Snap your legs toward the mat and push with your arms and shoulders to lift the upper portion of your body to an erect position. Allow your body weight to shift beyond the base. Put your hips back, swing your arms up and back, thrust your hips up and over, and extend from your legs. Put your hands on the mat. Let your legs and hips ride up to the vertical position. As your hips reach this position, break them and snap your legs down. Push with your arms and shoulders to raise the upper part of your body to an erect position for the back dive. As your feet land from the back handspring, swing your arms and head up and extend your legs and hips up in a back dive. Just before your hips reach the maximum flight going up, drop one shoulder and look in the same direction to execute a half twist. On the down swing, move your hips forward beyond the shoulders and place your hand on the mat. Duck your head and roll down the back of your neck, shoulders, and back to a forward roll recovery.

Common Errors:

(1) Having improper hand placement going into the round-off. (2) Executing a half turn in the round-off before your legs and hips reach the vertical. (3) Failing to allow your body weight to move beyond the base before extending your hips and swinging your arms and head back in the first part of the handspring. (4) Having inadequate thrust of your arms and shoulders and snap of your legs following the recovery of the back handspring. (5) Executing the half twist before your feet leave the mat on the back dive half twist. (6) Having an improper body position coming down for the landing in the forward roll.

Coaching Points:

(1) Place your hands in front of the drive leg and slightly in front of your shoulders on the round-off. (2) Do a half twist as your legs and hips reach the vertical position. (3) In the back handspring, allow your body weight to move beyond the base before extending your arms and head back and your hips up and over in the first part of the back handspring. (4) Do not begin the second phase of the back handspring until your legs and hips have reached the vertical position. (5) Following the back handspring lift your body up, swing your arms and head up, extend your legs, and drive your hips forward to get height in the direction of the back dive for the half twist. (6) Do a half twist after your body is in the air for the back dive. Be sure you have proper coordination of your hips and shoulders coming out of the roll.

Practice Hints:

(1) Review the standing back dive with a half twist and forward roll before doing the series. (2) Do a round-off, back handspring, back dive with a half twist on a foam pad before putting them on regular mats. (3) Work the back handspring, back dive with a half twist to a forward roll on the trampoline. (4) Use a spotter.

Spotting Tips:

The spotter stands to the side in front of you. As you run for the mat and place your hands down for the round-off, he places his first hand on your stomach while your legs and hips reach the vertical position executing a half turn. He then moves back, ready for your back handspring. He places his first hand on the small of your back and his second one behind your thighs. As you do the back hand-spring, he lifts upward the top portion of your body with his first hand while his second one lifts your thighs and legs upward to establish rotation. He moves back as you leap into the air. Both his arms en-compass your body in a cradle position as you do the back dive half twist. He holds your body in the cradle and allows you to land, softly, making sure that your hips, head, and shoulders are in proper position for a safe roll recovery.

78. Combination Front Somersault Stepout, Round-off, Back Handspring, Back Somersault Tuck

From a standing position facing the mat, take several running steps. Do a double-foot take-off. Swing your arms and head up and extend your leg from the mat. As your body rotates up, move your hips up. Swing your arms and head forward and down, tucking your knees tight to your chest and establishing a forward rotation. As your legs pass beyond the vertical position, extend one leg forward and allow the other one to come down under your body, executing a step-out. As you go into the round-off, place your hands in front of your shoulders and the drive foot. Swing your legs up to the vertical posi-tion and as they reach it, do a half turn. Snap your legs down and push from your arms and shoulders, allowing the top of your body to come up for the back handspring. Going into the back handspring, let your body weight move beyond the base. Extend your arms and head up and back. Thrust your hips up and drive your legs from the mat. As you place your hands on the mat, swing your hips and legs up to the vertical position. Snap your legs down. Push with your arms and shoulder to raise the top part of your body as your legs go down.

When you land out of the back handspring, lift your body forward and up by swinging your arms up and moving your head back. As your body leaves the mat, pull your knees to your chest. Keep your head back and swing your arms over, establishing back rotation. Keep your knees in tight to your chest for a tight tuck. As your body rotates back and your feet pass beneath your body, extend your legs from the tuck for the landing.

Common Errors:

(1) Not going up but out on the angle of take-off in the front somersault stepout. (2) Failing to split your legs at the proper time for the walkout from the front somersault. (3) Having improper arm placement in the round-off. (4) Not twisting your hips at the vertical in the round-off. (5) Not allowing your body weight to shift beyond the base before going into the handspring. (6) Swinging your arms and head back going into the back somersault rather than up in order to do a high tuck.

Coaching Points:

(1) Review the skills of a front somersault stepout. (2) Remember the proper hand placement on the round-off. (3) Do the half turn in the round-off as your legs and hips pass the vertical position. (4) Allow your body weight to shift beyond the base before extending your body for the back handspring. (5) Swing your arms and head up to get elevation and angle of flight before going into the back somersault tuck. (6) Tuck your knees tightly to your chest while rotating in the back somersault.

Practice Hints:

(1) Work the front somersault stepout, round-off, and back handspring before adding the tucked somersault. (2) Do the front somersault stepout off a stack of mats onto a lower level of them. Continue the rest of the combination on the regular level. Use the height in the beginning of the front somersault for rotation and position. (3) Use a spotter in the combinations of these skills.

Spotting Tips:

The spotter stands to the side in front of you. As you do the double-foot take-off going into the front somersault stepout, he places his first hand on your mid-section as you swing your arms up preparing to lift off the mat. As you lift your body, tuck your hand, and swing your arms forward and down, he places his second hand on the small of your back to aid you in rotation. He assists you until you complete the walkout and you move your body weight forward preparing to go into the round-off. As you place your hands down and bring your legs to the vertical, he places his first hand on your mid-section as you execute a half turn snapping down from the round-off. As your body weight passes beyond the base, his first hand goes to the small of your back and his second hand behind your thighs. As you extend your body up and over, his first hand gives direction and elevation to the top of your body while his second hand aids the extension of your hips and the rotation of your legs. As you swing your arms and head up, his first hand goes on the small of your back while his second hand goes beneath your hips. As you lift up, his first hand aids the elevation and flight of the top of your body while his second hand adds rotation to your hips by pushing them up and over.

79. Back Somersault with Full Twist

From a standing position with your back to the mat, swing your arms and head up and back, extend your hips forward and up, and drive your knees up to lift your body into the back dive. As your hips begin to go up, drop your head and shoulders to one side for the half twist. As your head and shoulders descend and your hips rise to their maximum height, you will see the mat. Allow your head and shoulders to go forward and down while twisting your hips to execute the half twist. Brandy out to the landing.

Common Errors:

(1) Having improper direction in the take-off, going back instead of up. (2) Executing the half twist in the first phase of the back dive before your feet leave the mat. (3) Doing the front somersault with a half twist before your hips reach the vertical position. (4) Failing to keep your head and shoulders turning in the same direction for the twisting.

Coaching Points:

(1) Swing your arms up and over, getting proper elevation before doing the half twist. (2) Drop your head and shoulders to the same side. (3) Break your hips violently as your legs start down at the end of the half twist in the front somersault.

Practice Hints:

(1) Work with a spotter when doing a back dive with a half twist to the forward roll. (2) Do the back dive with a half twist into the cradled arms of the spotter. When your hips pass the vertical position and your head points down, he helps you do another half twist the same way you would do a round-off, thereby completing the full turning process. (3) Work the back dive with a half twist, brandy out, full twisting somersault on the trampoline, using the extra flight for proper execution of this skill. (4) Use hand spotting while learning this skill.

Spotting Tips:

As you swing your arms and head up and extend your hips going into the back dive, the spotter cradles your body with both hands. As you do a half twist with your head coming down and your hips

Back Somersault with Full Twist

going to the vertical, his second hand moves from your mid-section, reaches around on top of your body, and places it beneath your mid-section after the half twist in the vertical position of the front somersault has been done. He aids you through the rest of the skill by supporting your body as needed.

80. Combination Round-off, Back Handspring, Back Somersault with Full Twist

From a standing position facing the mat, take several running steps and lift the drive leg forward. Bend from your hips and place your hand in front of your shoulders and drive leg. Put your first hand in front of the drive leg and your other one over behind the first. Throw your thrust leg up. As your hips and legs reach the vertical position, execute a half turn snapping your legs down toward the mat, and push with your arms and shoulders causing your body to rise to an erect position. When going into the back handspring, allow your body weight to move beyond the base. Swing your arms up, your head back, and extend your hips up and over as you place your hands down. Bring your hips and legs up to the vertical. Break your hips, snapping them down. Push with your arms and shoulders to raise your body to an erect position preparing for the back somersault with a full twist. Swing your arms up and over, dropping your head and shoulders to one side, to execute the back dive with a half twist. As your hips reach the vertical and your head starts down, do a brandy-out somersault by turning a half twist with your legs, snapping them down as in a round-off. Do a back dive with a half twist and brandy out to the landing.

Common Errors:

(1) Failing to place your hands in front of the drive leg going into the round-off. (2) Executing the half turn of your hips too soon when going into the round-off. (3) Failing to allow your body weight to move beyond the base before executing the back handspring by swinging your arms up and your head back while extending your hips. (4) Having an insufficient angle of take-off going into the back somersault with the half twist. (5) Failing to execute the back dive with the half twist. (6) Not having your legs and hips in the vertical position as you try to do the brandy-out somersault in the last phase of the full twist.

Coaching Points:

(1) Remember to place your hands down in front of the drive leg with both hands landing at the same time, the second hand around and behind the first one. (2) Execute a half twist as your legs and hips

pass the vertical position. (3) As your hips snap down, shove with your arms and shoulders to bring the upper part of your body to an erect position when coming out of the round-off to prepare for the back handspring. (4) In the first phase of the back handspring, allow your body weight to move beyond the base before extending your hips up and your arms and shoulders back. (5) Have the proper angle of take-off when coming out of the back handspring going into the back somersault with a full twist. (6) Do not begin the twist too soon. Wait until your body is suspended in the back dive before executing the half twist. When your hips pass over your head, do a half twist or brandy out.

Practice Hints:

(1) Review the mechanics of a back somersault with a full twist before doing the skill. (2) Work the back handspring and back somersault entirely on the trampoline. (3) Use a spotting belt when you do this skill for the first time.

Spotting Tips:

The spotter stands to the side and in front of you. As you run for the mat, he moves alongside as you go into the round-off. He does not help you unless you need it. He follows your body movement in the back handspring. He puts his first hand near the small of your back and his second hand beneath your body. He touches you only when necessary. When you go into the back somersault, full twist and lift-up, he extends both arms under your body so that you can do a back dive with a half twist into this cradle. As your body reaches the vertical position and you do a front somersault with a half twist out, his second hand comes from beneath your stomach and reaches around your body waiting to help you at the mid-section as you execute the full twist.

81. Combination Round-off, Back Handspring, Back Somersault with Whip-back, Back Handspring

From a standing position facing the mat, take several running steps. Lift your arms above your head and extend the drive leg forward. Bend from your hips placing both hands in front of the drive leg, the second one beyond the first. Throw your legs up. As your hips reach a vertical position, execute a half twist snapping your legs down and pushing from your shoulders to establish an upright position following the round-off. Allow your body weight to move beyond the base, sitting back for the back handspring. Swing your arms and head up and back as you extend your hips up and over. Shove your legs. As your hands touch the mat, bring your feet and legs to a vertical position. Break from your hips, snapping your legs down. Push with your arms and shoulder to establish an erect position out of the back handspring. Allow your body weight to move beyond the base. Swing your arms and head back and over. Extend your hips up and over pushing with your legs. Do not touch the mat with your hands. Snap your legs down as they reach the vertical position. Continue to move your body weight back as you finish the back whip, back somersault. As your body weight moves beyond the mass going into the last back handspring, swing your arms and head up and over while you extend your hips and shove from your legs. As your legs reach the vertical position, break from your hips and snap them down, then shove from your arms and shoulders to arrive at an erect position.

Common Errors:

(1) Having improper hand placement going into the round-off. (2) Executing the half twist of your hips in the round-off too soon. (3) Failing to allow your body weight to move beyond the base before exploding your hips, arms, and shoulders when going into the first phase of the handspring. (4) Lifting too much up and not enough back and over for the back somersault with whip-back. (5) Failing to allow your body weight to move beyond the base as you come out of the back somersault whip-back before going into the back handspring.

Coaching Points:

(1) Place your hands in front of your shoulders and the drive leg as you go into the round-off. (2) Execute a half twist with your legs and hips when they reach the vertical position. (3) Push from your arms and shoulders in the last phase of the handspring and round-off, allowing the top of your body to straighten. (4) Be sure the flight for the back somersault whip-back is up, not back to allow your hands to clear the mat as your legs whip over. (5) Keep your body weight moving out of the back somersault whip-back to go into the back handspring.

Practice Hints:

(1) Work from a standing position on the mat, doing the back handspring, back somersault whip-back, back handspring. Do these individually using a spotter. (2) Work the back handspring, back somersault whip-back on a trampoline to learn the proper mechanics. (3) Use a spotter when you do the series.

Spotting Tips:

The spotter stands to the side and in front of you. As you bend forward placing your hands down, going into the round-off, he stands close, ready to help you. He shifts back to protect you as you go into the back handspring. He puts one hand on the small of your back and the other one beneath your hips, to assist you as you go into the back whip-back. With the first hand he lifts your shoulders and he establishes rotation to whip your legs over. He checks to see if your body weight moves beyond the base before going into the back handspring. He spots it by placing his first hand on the small of your back and his second beneath your thighs. Again he aids the upward lift of your body and the extension and pushing of your legs down.

82. Combination Round-off, Back Handspring, Back Somersault Whip-back, Back Handspring, Back Somersault in Tucked Position

From a standing position facing the mat, take several running steps. Lift your arms above your head and extend the drive leg forward. Bend from your hips placing both hands in front of the drive leg. Put one hand in front of your legs while your other one reaches over and beyond the first one. Throw your legs up and, as your hips reach a vertical position, execute a half twist snapping your legs down and pushing from your shoulders to come to an upright position following the round-off. Allow your body weight to move beyond the base and sit back of the back handspring. Swing your arms and head up and back as your hips extend up and over, shoving from your legs. As your hands touch the mat, your feet and legs come to the vertical position. Break from your hips, snapping your legs down. Push with your arms and shoulders to establish an erect position after the back handspring, using no hands. Allow your body weight to move beyond the base. Swing your arms and head back and over. Extend your hips up and over, pushing with your legs. Do not touch the mat with your hands, and snap your legs down as they reach the vertical position. Continue to move your body weight back as you come out of the back whip-back somersault. As your body weight moves beyond the mass going into the last back handspring, swing your arms and head up and over, and extend your hips shoving from your legs. As your legs reach the vertical position, break from your hips and snap them down, while you shove from your arms and shoulders, arriving in an erect position during the alternate series. As your body lands erectly, swing your arms and head up, and extend your hips up and over. As your body leaves the mat, tuck your knees to your chest, allowing your body to rotate up and back going into the tuck somersault. As your hips and legs pass beyond the vertical position, continue to hold the tight tucked position until your legs are below your body pointing toward the mat. Extend from the tuck to prepare for the landing.

Common Errors:

(1) Having improper position of your hands in the round-off. (2) Twisting your hips in the first phase of the round-off after your legs

have passed the vertical position. (3) Failing to allow your body weight to move beyond the base before exploding your hips, shoulders, and arms in the first part of the back handspring. (4) Having inadequate thrust of your arms and shoulders as your hips snap down, causing the top of your body to return to an erect position when coming out of the back handspring. (5) Going *up* on your angle of flight, instead of back on the back handspring whip-back, thus causing your body momentum to be lost. (6) Allowing your body weight to move beyond the base before extending your arms, hips, and head as you go into the back handspring. (7) Going back instead of forward on your angle of flight in the back somersault tuck, as you rotate in the back tuck.

Coaching Points:

(1) Place your hands down slightly in front of your shoulder and in line with your drive leg going into the round-off. (2) Execute a half twist with your hips as your legs and hips reach the vertical position. (3) Allow your body weight to move beyond the base before exploding the mechanics of your arms, shoulders, and hips going into the first phase of the back handspring. (4) Allow your body weight to move back as you go into the back handspring whip-back, back somersault whip-back. Throw your head back, your arms up and over, while you throw your hips. Do not touch the mat with your hands in this series. When you land from the back somersault whip-back, be sure your body weight moves beyond the base before sitting back and lifting your arms, shoulders, and hips going into the back handspring. (5) When coming out of the back handspring, swing your arms and shoulders forward and up, put your head back, and extend your legs as your body comes off the mat. Tuck your knees to your chest, allowing your body to rotate up and over in the back somersault.

Practice Hints:

(1) From a standing position, do a back handspring, then a back somersault tuck. (2) Work the first part of the series with the aid of a spotter. (3) From a minitramp, do a back somersault and back handspring.

Spotting Tips:

The spotter stands to the side in front of you. As you bend forward and place your hands down when going into the round-off, he stands ready to aid you. He protects you as you go into the back handspring by putting his first hand on the small of your back and his second one beneath your hips. He assists you when going into the back whip-back by placing his first hand on the small of your back to lift your shoulders and his second hand beneath your hips to establish rotation by whipping your legs over. He checks to see whether your body weight moves beyond the base before going into the back handspring. He spots the back handspring by placing his first hand on the small of your back and his second one beneath your thighs. He aids the upward lift of your body and the extension and pushing of your legs down. In the back somersault tuck, he places his first hand on the small of your back as your hips extend up while your arms and head go back. He places his second hand behind your thighs giving lift to your hips and aiding your legs by establishing rotation as they reach the vertical and start down.

IV

RULES AND SCORING

Many methods are used to score tumbling. On the national level, the competitor is required to do three compulsory and four optional passes. Separate scores are given for them, then the two scores are totaled.

Often on the local level, the national requirements are waived. The rules are revised to best meet the needs of that particular meet.

V

TERMINOLOGY

Base. That part of the body which is in contact with the mat.

Body line. A prescribed position of the body while executing a skill.

Brandy out. A front somersault and a half twist with the eyes looking at the mat throughout the skill.

Center of gravity. The point of the body where the weight at the top and bottom is equal.

Down flight. That movement which takes place when the body is descending from its highest point for the landing.

Drive leg or foot. The one that is extended to push off from the mat.

Eye focus. That requirement of looking at a stationary object when one does a skill.

Frontal plane. That moment when the movement of the body is back and forth.

Hopping of hands. Quick movement of the hands forward on the mat in a front walkover.

Kinesthetic sense. The ability to know inwardly what one's body position is and what he must do to change it.

Layout. A basic body position created by the extension of the body from the toes to the head.

Momentum. That motion which is established by a previous movement.

Pike. A basic body position which is created by bending from the hips and lowering the top of the body toward the extended legs.

Puppet string method. A method involving the movement of several parts of the body in the same direction at the same time, as in puppetry.

Rocker. A curvature of the back and neck.

Scale. A succession or progression of steps.

Spiral rotation. That rotation which is done through the vertical.

Thrust or throw leg. The one that is extended and thrown up.

Straddle. An open stance position created by extending the legs to the side.

Tinsica. A front handspring with a cartwheel action, one hand being ahead of the other and the legs spread to make the spokes of a wheel.

Tuck. A basic body position created by rounding the back, tucking the knees to the chest, and bringing the feet to the seat.

Vertical plane. That time when the motion of the body is in an up and down direction.

VI

BIBLIOGRAPHY

Armbruster, Sr., David R., Irwin, Leslie W., and Musher, Frank J.: *Basic Skills in Sports for Men and Women*. St. Louis: The C. V. Mosby Company, 1967.

This text contains terse descriptions of many skills used in competitive events. The chapter on Rebound Tumbling is especially well done.

Drury, Blanche Jessen, and Schmid, Andrea Bodó: *Gymnastics for Women*. Palo Alto, California: The National Press, 1965.

This classic book should be part of the library of each gymnastic enthusiast. Of particular value is the section on gymnastics for women. The many illustrations included throughout the book help lead to greater reader understanding and appreciation of each intricate movement involved in gymnastics.

Loken, N. C., and Willoughby, R. J.: *Complete Book of Gymnastics*. Englewood Cliffs, New Jersey: Prentice Hall, Inc., 1967.

Slanted toward and written for the female gymnast. Both the performer and coach will benefit greatly from studying this well written text.

Norman, Randi: *Gymnastics for Girls and Women*. Dubuque, Iowa: Wm. C. Brown Company Publishers, 1965.

This well written booklet, although small in size, is big in value both to the performer and teacher of gymnastics.

Ruff, Wesley K.: *Gymnastics, Beginner to Competitor*. Dubuque, Iowa: Wm. C. Brown Company Publishers, 1959.

Competitors will be especially grateful for the availability of this book.

U.S. Naval Institute: *Gymnastics and Tumbling*. New York: The Ronald Press Company, 1959.

A standard reference which contains a wide variety of activities for men.

Yeager, Patrick: *A Teacher's Guide for Tumbling and Pyramids*. Statesboro, Georgia: Wide World Publications, 1963.

An invaluable reference for the teacher-coach of gymnastics.

VII

AVAILABLE FILM

A film, *Basic Tumbling*, includes the skills in the same sequence as they are in this booklet—elementary tumbling, the handstand, acrobatics, free tumbling, and aerials. The spotting techniques for each skill are also given.

This rents for twenty dollars a week. The fee includes postage and insurance. Available from Mr. Vannie M. Edwards, Physical Education Department, Centenary College, Shreveport, Louisiana.